Twayne's United States Authors Series

Sylvia E. Bowman, *Editor*

INDIANA UNIVERSITY

Sarah Orne Jewett

SARAH ORNE JEWETT

by RICHARD CARY
Colby College

Twayne Publishers, Inc.   .:   New York

MANUFACTURED IN THE UNITED STATES OF AMERICA BY
UNITED PRINTING SERVICES, INC.
NEW HAVEN, CONN.

For
FRANCES PERKINS CARY
A Maine Perennial

Preface

AMONG students of American regional literature *The Country of the Pointed Firs* is consistently awarded the palm as the best work of fiction on nineteenth-century rural New England. This has had the effect of unjustifiably reducing Sarah Orne Jewett to the dimensions of a one-book author. The danger is that of lost heritage. In the twenty volumes she turned out in her time are contained vital records of a unique people in a special circumstance. It is deplorable that only one paperback, which includes this novel and eleven of her short stories, is now generally available outside of libraries. A hopeful note is sounded in the announcement that an inexpensive edition of *Deephaven* is forthcoming.

One of the reasons for this misconception of Miss Jewett's productivity is the paucity of notice accorded by modern critics to her other works. By cleaving to "A White Heron" and "The Dulham Ladies," they and the anthologists perpetuate the impression that she wrote just two short stories. Her superb sketches are referred to with extreme rarity. (Most of these short stories and sketches are available in collected volumes, indicated in the *Selected Bibliography* at the end of this book.)

This study is an attempt to redress the balance and to bring back to light the buried excellences of Miss Jewett. Since no full critical review has ever been made of her work, six of the seven chapters are devoted to analysis of her materials, methods, and forms. Each sketch, short story, and novel is examined in relation to the long maturation of her genius and its own place as a work of literature. Each is regarded as a component of the mosaic in which *The Country of the Pointed Firs* is the principal and culminating motif.

Literary influences are at best *ignes fatui*, and no exertion has been made here to tie Miss Jewett inextricably to this author or that. Where English or European likenesses appear, they have been noted. Greater effort has been expended to remove her from the cubicle of local color and set her properly in the larger American frame. Her compassion for humanity, her vision of the external world, and her obeisance to the eternal verities earn her the more spacious place.

RICHARD CARY

Ocean Point
Maine

Contents

Chapter

    Chronology   11

1.   Grave New World   15

2.   Spinsters, Dignity, and the Dead Seaport   30

3.   Pastel in a Metal Frame   48

4.   Down the White Rose Road   65

5.   Technique and Temperament   87

6.   The Country of the Sad Captains   131

7.   The Remainder and the Reputation   155

    Notes and References   160

    Selected Bibliography   165

    Index   172

Chronology

1849   Born September 3, in South Berwick, Maine. Descendant of sea captains, traders, and physicians; daughter of a country doctor.

1855   Began desultory elementary education at Miss Raynes's school.

1856   Chronically ill throughout childhood; driving with her father on his daily rounds of patients, she spent less time in school than outdoors.

1863   Read Harriet Beecher Stowe's *The Pearl of Orr's Island*; resolved to portray Maine countryfolk with absolute verity.

1865   Was graduated from Berwick Academy.

1868   Frequent trips to Boston and New York; vacation of several months with her uncle's family in Cincinnati.

1868   First published short story, "Jenny Garrow's Lovers." Used pseudonyms "A. C. Eliot," "Alice Eliot" for several of her earliest pieces, and "Sarah O. Sweet" at least once.

1869   "Mr. Bruce," her first appearance in the *Atlantic Monthly*.

1872   Circle of friendships began to widen, including editors Horace E. Scudder, Thomas Bailey Aldrich, James T. Fields, William Dean Howells, and authors Lowell, Whittier, Holmes, Stowe, Henry James; in later years, Emerson, Longfellow, Cather.

1875   Trips to Philadelphia, Chicago, Wisconsin.

1877   Encouraged by Howells, she collected several early sketches to form her first volume, *Deephaven*.

1878   Death of her father, who had taught her about nature, people, and books, and to whom she dedicated *Country By-Ways* in 1881.

1880   Lifelong friendship established with Annie Fields; began spending part of each winter at her Boston home, and part of each summer at her Manchester-by-the-Sea cottage.

1882　First trip to Europe with Annie Fields. Visited Ireland, England, Norway, Belgium, Italy, France, Switzerland; met Tennyson, Charles Reade, Christina Rossetti.

1884　*A Country Doctor* published; fictive re-creation of her father and of her early ambitions for a medical career.

1886　"A White Heron" and "The Dulham Ladies" published.

1888　Vacation with Annie Fields in St. Augustine, Florida; inspired several stories with southern locale. "Miss Tempy's Watchers" published.

1889　Visited Alice Longfellow in the Boothbay region of the Maine coast, the general area she adopted six years later as the setting of *The Country of the Pointed Firs*.

1890　"The Town Poor" and "By the Morning Boat" included in *Strangers and Wayfarers*.

1892　Second trip to Europe with Annie Fields. Visited Italy, France, England; met Tennyson again, Mrs. Humphry Ward, George Du Maurier, Mark Twain.

1894　"The Guests of Mrs. Timms" published.

1896　Cruise of Caribbean islands with Annie Fields and the Aldriches. *The Country of the Pointed Firs* published.

1898　Third trip to Europe with Annie Fields. Visited France, England; met Kipling at Rottingdean, Henry James at Rye.

1900　Fourth trip to Europe with Annie Fields. Visited Italy, Greece, Turkey, France.

1901　*The Tory Lover* published, her only deliberate attempt at a dramatic novel. Received honorary Litt.D. degree from Bowdoin College, the first woman so honored.

1902　Seriously injured in fall from carriage on September 3. Never fully recovered her physical powers or literary capacity, but continued writing letters prolifically and visiting friends when her condition allowed.

1908　Spent much of the year with Annie Fields in Boston and Manchester-by-the-Sea.

1909　Died June 24, in South Berwick.

Sarah Orne Jewett

CHAPTER 1

Grave New World

B Y THE MIDDLE of the nineteenth century the town of South Berwick, Maine, was already living on memories. The natives reviled the remote Embargo of 1807 as Jefferson's folly and referred to the War of 1812 as "the last war." The clang of shipwrights' hammers and the hubbub of sailors at work or play had faded from the scene. In these lank years of a once prosperous and lively inland port, activity had come to a virtual halt. There was prospect in a mill, in a cannery, but the glory was departed. Into this aura of transfixed history Sarah Orne Jewett was born on September 3, 1849, and was to be gripped by the magic of its contours, chronicles, and characters throughout the nearly sixty years of her life.

The matter of influences which help to shape the personality or craft of an artist presents problems not usually resolved to everyone's satisfaction. In the case of Miss Jewett, Taine's familiar trinity of *la race, le milieu et le moment* offers an adaptable basis for procedure. Her cast of mind and the direction of her endeavor patently derived from the peculiar conjunction of her birth and development as a member of the benevolent aristocracy in the removed and rural state of Maine during a period of disheartening economic inertia.

I *The Changing Times*

The soil in this northern district begrudged subsistence and was insufficient for comfort. From the beginning, settlers gravitated toward the extended, contorted coastline. Shipping and shipbuilding emerged as the most promising routes to wealth. Starting modestly with American and European trade, venturous sea captains soon fanned outward to the West Indies, to India and China, and finally to every accessible port of call in the world's seven seas. Out of the mounting profits evolved a self-assured gentry not too proud to lend itself to a system of pliant, tacit class distinctions.

Two temblors, coming more than half a century apart, destroyed a way of life in Maine. The first shook it to its foundations; the second brought down the houses. Although they can be named and dated—the Embargo of 1807 and the Civil War—they were not distinct and isolated phenomena. Each incorporated a congeries of economic and social forces which would not be denied. The shifting accents of trade and the newer, unglamorous occupations had small appeal for imperturbable Mainers, who persisted in the routines of the past. In the long run, however, the inanimate stresses prevailed.

The Embargo, which lasted from December, 1807, to March, 1809, prohibited all commerce with foreign nations. This inspired immediate remonstrance from many New England communities which were certain that it was conceived as a diabolical plot to ruin them. For those whose livelihood was the sea, it posed a fine dilemma: to obey the law and accept privation or to violate it and risk arrest. Smuggling flourished but legitimate commerce drooped. When it became obvious that the Embargo would not bring France and England to their knees, the law was replaced by a Non-Intercourse Act which permitted trade with all nations save them. But the damage had been done. Goods rotted in warehouses, grass grew on the wharves, and sailors and longshoremen looked vainly for employment. Many ports in Maine never recovered from the blow.

A sharper jolt came with the end of the Civil War, which itself had drained from Maine a goodly quota of its youth. When the dust of the conflict settled, there came into clearer focus a multiplicity of factors which had been slowly altering the course of the nation's growth but which now assumed dominance with accelerated intensity. The lustiest facts of the new existence were industrialization and the proliferation of cities, with their concomitants of large-scale production, corporate organization, and diminishing individualism. Western frontiers beckoned to the bold, the ambitious, the frustrated. Burgeoning railroads furnished easy passage there as well as to manufacturing centers. Immigration rose prodigiously, creating unprecedented problems of human association in villages insulated for several generations. Least tolerable of all was the invasion of rural standards and manners by tastes engendered in the upsurging urban industrial plutocracy.

Unwilling spectator to a tragedy of regional obsolescence, Miss Jewett remarked this complex of strange and dangerous forces with polite horror. About a decade before she was born, New York City had established itself as the chief radial point for inland trade; before she was twenty, the Union Pacific had completed linkage of the entire United States. These aftermaths of the Embargo and the Civil War she eyed with equal disfavor. "From this inland town of mine there is no sea-faring any more," she wrote. "It is only a station on the railways, and it has, after all these years, grown so little that it is hardly worth while for all the trains to stop."[1] In an early sketch, "River Driftwood," she alluded dourly to "the destroying left hand of progress."

The new order impinged itself physically upon Miss Jewett's consciousness. Not a mile from her home sprang up textile mills and the jerry-built homes of immigrant Irish and French-Canadian laborers. Her instinctive sympathy went out to these untutored newcomers, but she could not help reacting according to her class and condition. She frowned at these excrescences of economic energy, so far removed from the gracile clipper ship, and sighed for return of a culture ruled by gentry and motivated by high-minded charity.

One other intrusive element that troubled Miss Jewett was the growing horde of summer visitors. She "was possessed by a dark fear that townspeople and country people would never understand one another," found it "not altogether reasonable when timid ladies mistook a selectman for a tramp, because he happened to be crossing a field in his shirt sleeves," and vowed in the name of Plato "to make them acquainted with one another." Indeed, to correct the false impression of "the caricatured Yankee of fiction, striped trousers, bell-crowned hat, and all," constituted one of her strongest motives toward a literary career.

These remarks from the 1893 Preface to *Deephaven* attest her recognition of the local-color vogue that dominated American fiction from 1870 to 1900. The great dispersion, brought about by the Civil War and abetted by the spread of railroads and industry, opened the eyes of Americans to the vast divergence between regions, particularly in the remoter sectors where old folkways had survived without visible modification. For three decades, while original institutions and mores were being swept away by a ruthless mechanical surge toward modernity, laureates of the deep South, the far West, the Mississippi Valley, the Middle Atlantic states, and New England, depicted with determined pseudo-realism the picturesque and peculiar attributes of their respective localities. The tendency in most of this writing was to stress the special, the quaint, the primitive, and the idiosyncratic, at the expense of the common. Because the former qualities were fast passing into extinction, the nostalgic effort to preserve them in their primary colors often resulted in exaggeration and superficiality. Aspects of landscape, character, dialect, and manners were presented with an eye to their astonishing uniqueness and with an unstated protest against rising standardization. The aim was to set before the outside world memorable portraits of exceptional enclaves of people living out distinctive lives against backgrounds of singular beauty or bleakness.

Although Miss Jewett's expressed purpose was to inform the world about her home district and its inhabitants, she is not a local colorist pure and simple. She portrays indigenous scenes, characters, and customs, with native perspicuity and understanding; she only occasionally casts a romantic sheen over her materials. She does not merely describe, she works into the texture of her descriptions reserves of knowledge and experience drawn from long and sensitive intimacy with her milieu. She construes environment as a pictorial backdrop, but also as a powerful determining influence. She does not resort to blatant misspellings in idiom and dialect. Some of her people are unquestionably quaint or queer, but they also have a strong streak of the universal—George Quint, for instance, or William Blackett. Instead of yielding to the richness of these elements, she handles them with wise authority. Fidelity to vision and tranquility of tone earmark her method. It has brought her accolades from many quarters.

II *The Place and the People*

The foregoing factors which, directly or indirectly, affected Miss Jewett's thinking and writing originated principally outside her geographical domain. Other factors, fundamentally more profound and enduring, were transmitted through her immediate family and environs.

Sarah Jewett grew up in a spacious white clapboard house which in air and in architecture was strongly colonial. The majestic central staircase, the pulpit window of flowered glass, the gleaming mahogany bedsteads, and the predominance of Chippendale and Wedgwood pieces were all in approved British taste. Despite the achieved political freedom, New England at this time was still spiritually subservient to the mother country. "For many years," she notes in *Country By-Ways*, "New England was simply a bit of Old England transplanted. . . . If one of our own elderly ladies were suddenly dropped into the midst of provincial English society, she would be quite at home."[2] These vestiges of an older culture appealed to her conservative spirit and her sense of the value of the past. It delighted her to discover that the people in Jane Austen's novels were not unlike those she knew years ago in her own area. The social atmosphere to which she became accustomed in South Berwick was less Puritan than Anglican; it was marked by grace rather than regimen, tolerance rather than rigidity. Within these warm traditions she developed into a snug but not smug Brahmin lady.

Two significant traits may be connected with this eventuation: intellectually, her fondness for re-creating the past; emotionally, her regressive desire to remain a child. An unquenchable urge for things-as-they-were, for the olden golden days of simplicity and serenity, informs the great bulk of her work. She abhors the abrasive race for money and power; she regards with alarm the multiplying complexities of the machine age. Reluctant to wrestle with the new realities, she exclaims at the age of forty-eight, "This is my birthday and I am always nine years old."[3] Earlier she had complained to Howells that "everybody is distressingly grown-up and I have 'nobody to play with.' "[4] Her continuing will to live in a state of suspended naïveté is notable in her insistence upon adolescent nicknames, in her puerile effusions "to indicate great joy,"[5] and in Annie Fields's revelation that "she never put her doll away." In these ineffectual ways she tried to turn back and hold back the hands of the clock. Writing on the death of Longfellow, she acknowledges unwilling surrender to "the demon of change" and cites the passing of older generations as the saddest aspect of the inevitable: "After all, it is change that is so hard to bear, change grows every year a harder part of our losses. It is fitting over our old selves to new conditions of things, without the help of the ones who made it easier for us to live, and to do our best that is so hard."[6]

Miss Jewett's dependence upon male elders is not to be understated. At least three men of her own family left positive imprints upon her dilating mind. There was her paternal grandfather, Theodore Furber Jewett, who ran away in his boyhood to ship on a whaler and underwent some unusual experiences. He later captained a vessel which defied the Embargo, was captured by the British and confined on the notorious Dartmoor Prison Ship. In the general store which he established on Berwick's Main Street in his retiring years the little girl sat, and from day to day heard an endless string of yarns from the Captain and his bevy of aging cronies. The saline flavor of these men and the traditions they had lived by bit deeply into her blood. Accepting the praise of a friend for not having made the people of *Deephaven* ridiculous, she explained in part, "I like to be with them. *Deephaven* is not the result of careful study during one 'summer's vacation,' as some persons have thought. . . . And as for the sailors; I have always known them. . . . When I was a child the Captains used to come to see my grandfather."[7]

There was also her maternal grandfather, Dr. William Perry of Exeter, New Hampshire, a man quite as stirring and substantial. In his youth he relinquished his right to the family farm, gained entry to the Harvard Medical School, and earned his degree. The rest of his life he spent healing the sick, inventing surgical devices, and racing spirited horses (until his late eighties) along neighboring beaches. His chief value to a naturally indolent girl was to perk her into action. He plied her with books, demanded reports, and made blunt comments on her responses. "[He was] always showing me where good work had been done, and insisting upon my recognition of the moral qualities that led to achievement."[8] Out of gratitude to his wisdom and incitement, she dedicated *The Story of the Normans* to him.

No man in Miss Jewett's life, however, so thoroughly and variously inspired her as did her father, Dr. Theodore Herman Jewett. Countryside general practitioner and author of articles in medical journals, his combination of practicality and scholarship proved invaluable in orienting his gifted daughter in two directions. Through his acquaintance with nature and his insight into people he led her to appreciate the abundance of the present;

through his knowledge of books and history he infused her with veneration for the wealth and sinew of the past. She inscribed *Country By-Ways* "To T. H. J., my dear father; my dear friend; the best and wisest man I ever knew; who taught me many lessons and showed me many things as we went together along the country by-ways." Further attestation of her love may be descried in the portrait of Dr. Leslie in *A Country Doctor,*[9] and in the first two poems of *Verses,* so poignantly expressive of her loss when he died.

"The best of my education was received in my father's buggy and the places to which it carried me," she said to an interviewer.[10] Sickly in childhood, Sarah Jewett would skip school with "the wicked connivance" of her father and accompany him on his professional rounds. The joy of what she learned on these truant trips more than compensated for the prickings of her New England conscience. As they drove over rutted roads to seacoast shacks and inland farmhouses he pointed out with the skill of a botanist and zoologist the wonders of nature. Before long the child had absorbed every detail of plant and animal life within the circumference of their travels. "Now, as I write my sketches of country life, I remember again and again the wise things he said, and the sights he made me see."

While her father treated his patients, she watched and listened, often wandering off to talk to others in the household or on the grounds. Thus she came "in contact with many delightful men and women of real individuality and breadth of character, who had fought the battle of life to good advantage, and sometimes against great odds." Afterward she questioned her father about them and drank in his tales of their activities and aspirations, their oddities and sorrows.

Continuously he spoke to her about books. Although he dangled the advantages of Sterne, Fielding, Smollett, and Cervantes before her, she then seemed more amenable to Jane Austen, George Eliot, and Mrs. Oliphant. Gradually she came to admire Milton, Dr. Johnson, Arnold, Tennyson, and some of the seventeenth-century metaphysical poets; the Americans Emerson and Lowell; the French Zola, Montaigne, Balzac, and Flaubert; and the Russians Tolstoi and Turgenev. Her father's ardent concern with human beings and his passion for direct observation kept her from drifting into mere bookishness. At first perplexed, she later realized why he habitually reverted her gaze to familiar persons and places. "Don't try to write *about* people and things," he would say; "tell them just as they are!"

III *Her Emerging Consciousness*

On her own Sarah Jewett sought and imbibed generative experiences. In the immense garden that surrounded the Berwick mansion she savored the delights of elm and poplar, of lilacs, lilies, and pink hollyhocks. As she grew older, she ranged afoot over regional shores and fields and woods, avidly questing for odors of balsam, for spume-like marsh rosemary, for thrushes and butterflies. She walked up tangled paths to peer into forsaken farmhouses and wonder about the fate of departed families. "One may travel at home in a most literal sense, and be always learning history, geography, botany, or biography—whatever one chooses." A lifelong lover of horses, she began to take extended rides and drives, coming to know better the up-country people she had seen as a child in the village, carting lumber, hay, and produce to barter for tea, raisins and molasses. She dallied in the busy country stores, absorbing the cadences of pure country talk as Synge was later to do in the Aran Islands. Inexhaustible for impressions, she pried into fisheries and factories—"There is always something to be traced or discovered, something particularly to be remembered. One grows rich in memories and associations."[11]

Sarah Jewett's schooling was at best haphazard. She attended for some years a day school in town which the Misses Raynes ran, largely on the basis of individual instruction. She displayed a small talent for composition but no spark of superior scholarship. In 1861 she entered Berwick Academy, an old private school, went to classes desultorily for four years, and was graduated in 1865. This was the extent of her formal education. She seems never to have applied herself diligently to studies nor to have relished the shackles of schoolroom discipline. What she learned from books was mostly acquired from the ample shelves in her father's house and from her subsequent insatiable reading.

Few artists recognize the moment when the first impulse to create quivers within. More will remember the compulsion to create in a particular medium which suddenly becomes indisputable to them as a personal expression. In her letters and public writings Miss Jewett indulges in some minor introspections con-

cerning the creative process, but she makes no really illuminating
exposures, nor does she try to pinpoint the earliest flickering
desire to write. Responsive to her father's counsels, she does indicate a book and a current condition which conspired to channel
her esthetic energies. The book that initially moved her was
Harriet Beecher Stowe's *The Pearl of Orr's Island* (1862),
which she read when thirteen or fourteen; the condition, the
miscomprehension of natives by summer boarders, which she
became aware of when fifteen.

She could not forget "the exquisite flavor and reality of delight"
she derived from Mrs. Stowe's sympathetic delineation of the
lives of fisherfolk "along the wooded seacoast and by the decaying, shipless harbors of Maine." At forty, she thought it "as clear
and perfectly original and strong" as it had seemed in her teens.
There is of course no mystery to the attraction; *The Pearl of
Orr's Island* is in the vanguard of local-color literature. It "gave
the young author of 'Deephaven' to see with new eyes, and to
follow eagerly the old shore paths from one gray, weatherbeaten
house to another," but it did not overwhelm her to the extent
of obscuring its weaknesses. She determined to pursue the course
set by Mrs. Stowe, with as much compassion surely, but with
sturdier realism. "Alas, that she couldn't finish it in the same
noble key of simplicity and harmony."[12]

The actualities of time and place that propelled Miss Jewett
into verbal utterance are condensed in these three sentences
culled from her remarks to a Boston journalist:

> When I was, perhaps, fifteen, the first "city boarders" began
> to make their appearance near Berwick; and the way they
> misconstrued the country people and made game of their pe-
> culiarities fired me with indignation. I determined to teach the
> world that country people were not the awkward, ignorant set
> those people seemed to think. I wanted the world to know their
> grand, simple lives; and, so far as I had a mission, when I first
> began to write, I think that was it.[13]

The success of her father's prescriptions could receive no firmer
testimonial: she would get at truth by observing the facts and
interactions of real life, and by evoking a mood of human understanding through her written word. It is regrettable that her
feminine reticence and her adoration of the past somewhat
blurred the edges of her intent.

In her most deliberate autobiographical essay, "Looking Back on Girlhood," she recalls beginning to write down things she was thinking about while still a child. At first she found prose veritably terrifying, and so expressed herself in rhymes. When such poetry eventually became formidable, she shifted into the "more and more enticing" cadences of prose. By 1867 she was regularly submitting examples in both forms to children's magazines under pseudonyms (Alice Eliot, A. C. Eliot, Sarah O. Sweet) because, she explained, she was too shy to have it known even at home that she was writing.

Her first story, a cliché-ridden melodrama called "Jenny Garrow's Lovers," was published four months after her eighteenth birthday. Her first noteworthy success, however, came in December, 1869, with the appearance of her short story "Mr. Bruce" in the *Atlantic Monthly* under the personal auspice of William Dean Howells, then assistant to editor James T. Fields. From the next year on, her byline was seen with increasing frequency, first in such periodicals as *Riverside Magazine*, the *Independent, St. Nicholas,* and later in the *Atlantic, Harper's* and *Scribner's.* At Howells' impulsion, she collected several of her sketches about Maine, endowed them with a fictional frame, and presented them to the public in 1877 as her first book, *Deephaven.* The subject matter and her circumspect treatment of it captured immediate attention. Thereafter she was assured a wide and cordial audience for a career which lasted another twenty-five years and produced nineteen more volumes.

IV *Her Wider Associations*

The portrait of Sarah Orne Jewett thus far outlined—a self-taught provincial with uncommon perception and a gift of language—suffices for many. She was not, however, a single-sided naïve, nor was she a detached Janeite whose whole essence was contained within the boundary lines of a vicarage. While never a cosmopolite, Miss Jewett was well traveled and could summon up a roster of friendships extending far beyond the small corner of Maine which constituted her esthetic realm. She early became accustomed to prolonged visits with family friends in Boston. With something of the verve of her seafaring forebears she made numerous forays to New York, Cincinnati, Philadelphia, and one summer to the then far-west Wisconsin. As she grew in literary reputation, she broadened her scope of geographical excursions and widened her sphere of eminent acquaintances. In both these respects she owed much to her deepening relationship with Annie Fields, wife of Boston publisher James T. Fields.

Annie Fields, cultured, urbane, and fifteen years older than Miss Jewett, was instantly attracted to the simple, vivacious novice from the hinterlands. By 1880 Sarah was a consistent guest at the Fields summer home in Manchester-by-the-Sea, a north-shore Massachusetts town. The two women's mutuality of interest in reading, writing, and the arts provided a bond which strengthened considerably after the death of Mr. Fields in the following year. The almost inseparable duo of Mrs. Fields and Miss Jewett was thenceforth a familiar sight to their contemporaries. Miss Jewett spent part of each summer at the cottage on Thunderbolt Hill and of each winter at 148 Charles Street, Mrs. Fields's Boston residence. They not only read and wrote in charming harmony but entertained many of the famous authors who had come within the ken of Fields's publishing activities.

Together they took four trips to Europe in 1882, 1892, 1898, and 1900. Sarah Jewett wrote back enthusiastic impressions of England, Norway, Belgium, France, Switzerland, and Italy; she described the beauties of Ireland to her grandfather Perry, the classic landscapes and flowering fields of Greece to Mrs. Whitman, and the exotic allure of Constantinople to a youthful reader of *Betty Leicester*. She fairly exulted in her opportunities to meet Charles Reade, Tennyson, the Dickens family, Thackeray's daughter, Mark Twain in Venice, Mrs. Humphry Ward, George Du Maurier and his sprightly little dog, Christina Rossetti, Matthew Arnold's family, Henry James at Rye, and Kipling at Rottingdean. Closer to home, she and Mrs. Fields vacationed intermittently in St. Augustine, Florida, soaking up the sunshine and the heterogeneous demeanor of life. In the spring of 1896, accompanied by the Thomas Bailey Aldriches, they voyaged in the yacht of a friend through the Caribbean Sea, touching at Nassau, Inagua, and other islands.

In childhood she prized the companionship of elderly men; in adulthood her intimate friendships were predominantly feminine. Many of these were of course based upon social and temperamental congeniality, and their artlessly passionate quality may be judged from the correspondence which signalized and nurtured them. In varying degrees Miss Jewett also consorted with

ranking female writers of her time—Celia Thaxter, Susan Cool-
idge, Julia Ward Howe, Alice Meynell, Th. Bentzon (Madame
Marie Thérèse Blanc, the French critic and translator), Willa
Cather, Harriet Prescott Spofford, Vernon Lee, Louise Imogen
Guiney, and Harriet Beecher Stowe.

Although Miss Jewett remained unmarried all her life and
seems not to have had a single serious *affaire de coeur,* she established and sustained affable relationships with scores of men.
Some originated through her visits to their wives or daughters,
others through reciprocal literary and professional interests. The
record of long and germinative fellowship with the successive
editors of the *Atlantic Monthly* may be read in series of published and unpublished letters: Lowell, who liked to tease this
attractive young rustic; Fields; Howells, whose discrimination
introduced her to a national audience; Aldrich, with whom she
exchanged puns and persiflage; Scudder, who had given her
prior encouragement while editing the *Riverside Magazine;*
Page; and Bliss Perry. Other editors with whom she enjoyed
fruitful association included Henry M. Alden (*Harper's*), Robert
Underwood Johnson (*Century*), William Hayes Ward (*Independent*), and Lyman Abbott (*Outlook*).

Holmes and Longfellow she knew and honored. Her fraternity
with Charles Dudley Warner fostered the suggestion that she
write *The Tory Lover.* But it was with Whittier that she felt
most at home. She called at his Amesbury home and enjoyed
protracted talks with him about everything under the sun. They
communicated with each other while she was in this country
and abroad. On the occasion of her first trans-Atlantic sailing
he proffered the sonnet "Godspeed," to which she presently
responded with "The Eagle Trees." He eulogized the purity and
simplicity of *Deephaven* in a heartfelt note, and in 1888 she
dedicated *The King of Folly Island* to him "with grateful affection."

The nature of Miss Jewett's activities during a score of winters
spent in Boston added another dimension to the sophistication
she acquired through travel and eminent friendships. In that
city's heyday as America's cultural capital she moved through
a brilliant round of luncheons and dinners side by side with the
mightiest lions of the time. She attended art exhibits, music
recitals, theatrical performances, and the inevitable lectures. Now

and then she found time to join Mrs. Fields in her organizational and philanthropic projects, avoiding too precise involvement but gradually perceiving the social import of participation. She boated, drove, and week-ended with the families of benevolent magnates, and came to understand some of the sorcery of corporate business. She even learned to invest her money tidily.

It becomes evident that Sarah Jewett was no second Thoreau, who could elicit inside the precincts of Concord all he required to know and live by. Although the elements really valuable in her work stem from her sure knowledge of the circumscribed area she was born and grew up in, she felt a definite need for replenishment from external sources. Subconsciously she avoids the thin particularization that marks most local-color writing and bears down on the universal grain that underlies the veneer. To Willa Cather she unequivocally states her credo, "Of course, one day you will write about your own country. In the meantime, get all you can. One must know the world *so well* before one can know the parish."[14]

V *Death and the Tradition*

At the 1901 commencement exercises, Bowdoin College awarded Miss Jewett the degree of Litt.D., the first it had ever conferred upon a woman. Her pen spluttered excitedly as she depicted for Annie Fields the thrill of being "the single sister to so many brothers." From this apex of elation she was soon to be thrust, however, by the most calamitous event in her life since her father's passing. On the afternoon of September 3, 1902, her fifty-third birthday, she was thrown from a carriage when the horse tripped and fell over a loose stone. The injuries to her head and spine drastically curtailed her normal pursuits. She read, but not without spells of dizziness; she tried to write but experienced extreme difficulty (only two brief pieces presumably written after her accident were published in more than six years). She did a little walking, a little sailing, a little traveling, but her vigor and buoyancy were extinct. While at Mrs. Fields's Charles Street home, Miss Jewett was leveled by a stroke in March, 1909. She was transported to South Berwick where, three months later, she died in the house of which she had once said, "I was born here and I hope to die here."

Sarah Orne Jewett rose upon the New England literary scene in the lingering autumn of its most distinguished era. The reigning pentad of Emerson, Longfellow, Lowell, Holmes, and Whittier—all born at least a generation before her—had already published the works which endeared them to the American reading public and which are today considered their best. The power of the awesome tradition they had founded was enough to support them through three decades following the Civil War, during which they continued almost automatically to produce acceptable, but not comparable, prose and verse. Emerson slowly subsided into senility; Longfellow's *Kéramos* (1878) and *Ultima Thule* (1880) could not sufficiently revive the paling glow; Lowell served in successive posts of minister to Spain and to England from 1877 to 1885; Holmes's *A Mortal Antipathy* (1885) demonstrated his diminishing effectiveness as a novelist; and Whittier, with *Snow-Bound* and abolition behind him, turned increasingly to sentimentalized colonial history and bucolic idylls.

Into this twilight of dissolving memories strode a host of female authors, all eager to prolong the established Brahmin aura, yet sensible of the raw-toned realism emanating from beyond the Adirondacks and from the backwaters of the South. Among the "final legatees of Puritanism" nominated by Fred Lewis Pattee as "Recorders of the New England Decline" are Louisa May Alcott, Elizabeth Stuart Phelps, Helen Hunt Jackson, Celia Thaxter, and Sarah Orne Jewett.[15] This is doing Miss Jewett something of an injustice. She was indeed one of the peripheral figures who viewed the recent Golden Age with deference; but, unlike most of this group, she abstained from exploitation and sentimental excess.

Although self-schooled in the traditions that animated her New England predecessors, Miss Jewett is not nearly so derivative. She relies far less upon her library; and, even more acutely than Whittier, she searches herself and her surroundings for materials to transpose into literature. "There are still a good many examples of the old manner of out-of-door life and customs, as well as a good deal of the old-fashioned provincial society, left in the eastern parts of the New England states,"[16] she says. From a love of venerable neighbors, from a legion of anecdotes about departed days, from heartbreaking vistas of defunct farms and rotting wharves, she derived her prime desire

—to preserve the spirit of a splendid past and to laud the values of what remained.

By 1873 the impulse awakened by Mrs. Stowe's vignettes of native life had matured, and Sarah Jewett was determined in her course. "I am getting quite ambitious and really feel that writing is my work—my business perhaps; and it is so much better than making a mere amusement of it as I used."[17] She outgrew her perturbations about writing, and improved steadily in selectivity and control of her medium. From the tentative drawings of *Deephaven* (1877) to the hardier art of *A White Heron and Other Stories* (1886), one can chart the ascending confidence of a now-dedicated artist. *The Country of the Pointed Firs* came a decade later. With this book her reputation was insured. Not even her last attempt at a formal novel, *The Tory Lover* (1901), could impair it. After sixty years Sarah Orne Jewett still appeals to readers and critics as "mistress of an art of fiction all her own,"[18] a judgment which Henry James, master of an art of fiction all his own, could unhesitatingly make.

CHAPTER 2

Spinsters, Dignity,
and the Dead Seaport

G IVEN HER TEMPERAMENT, and also the time and the place in which she was born, Sarah Jewett's literary bearing is inescapable. She stands on the fringe of an era whose codes and rituals enthrall her, regrets its air of spiritual depletion, and determines to bring back to life—as far as pen and ink can—the simplicity and the strength that once underlay its daily existence. To this resolve she adds the aim of correcting the ludicrous misimpressions that cityfolk have of countryfolk. These gigantic tasks of revival and interpretation she takes upon herself out of devout love. Steeped in the ethos of her native past and present, she sees no need to distort or embroider. "Real life's interestin' enough for me," she has Abby Harran say in "A Native of Winby." So she paints no extravagant pictures, nor does she interject grotesques for their own sakes.

Meticulously and without ado, Miss Jewett, with an art perhaps too serene to appeal to the uninformed city audiences she had in mind, superimposes upon each other two worlds—one lost and one misunderstood. The most frequent criticism of her rendition is that she screens out of it all the coarse and contemptible actualities of life in favor of a too pervasive charm and refinement. She is accused of feminine fastidiousness, aristocratic bias, esthetic myopia, and downright ignorance. Her depictions of locale are condemned as idyllic and many of her characters cited as paragons of purity. She is very generously excused on the score that, while aware of the starker sides of existence, she deliberately evades them out of fidelity to her purpose of bringing out only the best.

A close examination of Sarah Jewett's world will reveal that none of these criticisms is entirely justified. She does not uniformly dulcify her scenes, nor do her people invariably demonstrate redeemable virtues. She knows the ugly underside of nature as minutely as its happier facets, and she seldom shrinks from presenting the despicable in human motives or behavior.

Miss Jewett's readers are continuously bemused by the lambency of descriptive passages such as those in the first pages of "By the Morning Boat," in chapters IX and XXI of *The Country of the Pointed Firs,* or in the rambling paragraphs of "The Confession of a House-Breaker." Teeming with sunlight and cinnamon roses, birdsong and ocean vistas, calm skies and titan pines, they tend to lull the senses and divert the mind from her more somber contemplations of Maine landscape. Not so prevalent as the brighter scenes, the grimmer ones nevertheless appear in her earliest work and are notable intermittently throughout her sketches and stories. Three or four miles out of Deephaven "the land was so poor that even the trees looked hungry." In "A Winter Drive" she acknowledges the "bare, thin, comfortless aspect of nature which is chilling to look at." In "The Courting of Sister Wisby" she gives ampler evidence of observing and understanding nature's capacity for cruel duplicity: "Every living thing grows suddenly cheerful and strong; it is only when you catch sight of a horror-stricken little maple in swampy soil, —a little maple that has second sight and foreknowledge of coming disaster to her race,—only then does a distrust of autumn's friendliness dim your joyful satisfaction."

In respect to characters, Miss Jewett does offer a surfeit of angels such as Nancy Gale, of formidable isolates who can be depended upon to thaw at the first show of human kindness, of remarkably meritorious children like little French Mary, and of dispossessed sea captains cheerfully dauntless to the last. On the other hand, Miss Jewett does not scant the meaner traits. Lightly, she defends the function of gossip as a social instrument in lonely, secluded hamlets, but in the persons of Mrs. Meeker (*A Country Doctor*) and Mrs. Corbell ("Miss Peck's Promotion") she scores the abusive intent that goes with so much of it. As counterweights to Debby Gaines, the sacrificial spinster in *An Empty Purse,* stand rude, shrewd, selfish Persis Flagg and impregnable Mrs. Timms, who act as flint and steel against each other in "The Guests of Mrs. Timms."

Not every heart dissolves over the adversities of Miss Jewett's protagonists. Having made his cunning bargain with John Packer in "A Neighbor's Landmark," Ferris is not moved by any consideration of Packer's emotional dilemma or the community's need. In "The Night Before Thanksgiving" John Mander exhibits no admirable attributes. Greedy for the helpless widow Robb's property, he cheats her, reproaches her for having been generous to worthless people, and advises her to go to the poorhouse. But Miss Jewett touches the raw core of human baseness in Sam Westcott, the craven neighbor who brings about the ruin of lovable, unassuming David Berry by pressing for payment of a $16 debt; Westcott does so not for the puny sum involved but for the satisfaction of showing Berry up "as no better than other folks."

Nor does Miss Jewett avert her eyes entirely from the depressive atmosphere or the seamy situations one is apt to encounter along shore or in the country. An early example occurs in the circus chapter of *Deephaven*. Kate and Helen are spared none of the squalor behind the spangles; they are made to listen to a protracted recital of the professional fat woman's pathetically hopeless career. Later they are exposed to a miasma of meanness and recrimination at the funeral of the impoverished widower. The plight of wistful Phebe Quint, unfortunate in her "hard-worked, New England plainness," mortally ill, and doomed by her father's deranged vow of self-banishment, infects "The King of Folly Island" with an unrelieved air of despondency. Except for the irate optimism of Mrs. Trimble, the same is true of the pitiable circumstances in "The Town Poor." The opening scene of "Farmer Finch" creates a mood of despair so enveloping that only the potency of a Polly Finch can conceivably dissipate it. And even in stories for children—"The Best China Saucer" and "Woodchucks"—Miss Jewett injects instances of juvenile spite, callosity, and sadism which writers of this genre carefully eschew.

In view of these and other veins of acute realism, one must reject the glib attribution of *idyllic* to Miss Jewett's re-created world. That this impression persists is due as much to the reader's desire for escape as to the author's preference for repose. High among Miss Jewett's articles of faith are belief in the fabled tranquility of the past, in the genteel acceptance of one's lot—good or grim, and in the ineradicable benevolence of humankind. It is not deficiency of art or vision that impels her to stress the buoyant over the dire experience. It is a matter of maidenly decision. Her training and status lend substance to the view that life is on the whole a sequence of pleasantly muted interchanges, only occasionally obstructed by enmity or irreparable tragedy. She sees life in its variegated shades but, secure in her conviction that happiness is the highest moral purpose, she selects her tints to suit herself.

Matthiessen comes to the conclusion that she is well aware of the bleak in nature and the sordid in man but "simply did not emphasize them." Frost essentially agrees that it is man's highest common denominator, not his lowest, that she seeks. Even Parrington, so brusque with Poe and Henry James, gallantly grants that Sarah Jewett makes a conscious choice based on "a Brahmin temperament."[1] A creature of heart rather than head, she finds such arresting parallels between herself and Stepniak's commentary on Turgenev that she copies out a full paragraph for a letter to Charles Miner Thompson:

> But there was in him such a love of light, sunshine, and living human poetry, such an organic aversion to all that is ugly, or coarse, or discordant, that he made himself almost exclusively the poet of the gentler side of human nature. On the fringe of his pictures, or in their background, just for the sake of contrast, he will show us the vices, the cruelties, even the mire of life. But he cannot stay in these gloomy regions, and he hastens back to the realms of the sun and the flowers, or to the poetical moonlight of melancholy, which he loves best because in it he can find expression for his own great sorrowing heart.[2]

The question of truth intrudes here. Can Sarah Jewett meet the test of reality with so decided an inclination? Does the social distance between herself and her subjects militate against genuine comprehension of their secret and subtle responses? The answer lies in the unshakeable authenticity of her collective portrayal.

She allows no barriers to stand between herself and her basic materials. She takes every advantage of the democratic fluency between classes in the area to absorb intimate reactions at the farther end of the scale. Forty years of transit through the wider world of culture failed to take the country out of her. She moves with the discretion of a more fortunate sister or daughter among the citizens of her region, protectively colored by her native knowledge of formalities and language. Beginning in childhood, she acquired a fathomless understanding of the works and ways of her neighbors through close and impulsive intercourse. And she has the gift of empathy. Sharing their monolithic religious faith and uncomplicated graph of values, their naïve pleasures and antipathies, she can slip without discomposure into their very identities.

Quite frequently Miss Jewett assumes the role of detached spectator in her sketches and stories, but this is a tactic to secure the benefits of an added point of view. This device of course contributes texturally to her success in imbuing her reconstructed world with a sense of verity. But the qualities which pre-eminently mould her art into a likeness of life are her elemental knowledge of and sympathy with "the country out of which I grew, and where every bush and tree seem like my cousins!"[3]

Against the indictment that she restricts her range too severely and deals with matters of negligible importance, Miss Jewett provides a number of retorts. During a perusal of epitaphs in Deephaven's burying ground, the narrator reflects: "It is wonderful, the romance and tragedy and adventure which one may find in a quiet old-fashioned country town, though to heartily enjoy the every-day life one must care to study life and character, and must find pleasure in thought and observation of simple things, and have an instinctive, delicious interest in what to other eyes is unflavored dulness."

In the first paragraph of "A Late Supper" Miss Jewett amplifies this subsurface perception of village life into an inclusive microcosmic theory. Speaking directly to the reader about Brookton, an inconspicuous town in the mountain region, she declares that "life is as important and exciting there as it is anywhere; and it is like every other town, a miniature world, with its great people and small people, bad people and good people, its jealousy and rivalry, kindness and patient heroism."

Not content with these generalized revelations about a condition obvious to her, and perhaps uncertain that her sketches and stories are demonstrating it effectively, Miss Jewett presses the point on several other occasions. In *A Country Doctor*, Dr. Ferris exclaims at the misconception about "prosaic" life in New England. In "Law Lane" it is noted that the comedies and tragedies of life are played as much by country people in homespun as by townsfolk in velvet and lace. In *Betty Leicester* the young heroine cries out, "Why, papa, dear, I do believe that there is one person in Tideshead of every kind in the world."

The strongest iteration of this truism, however, comes in the peroration of "A Landless Farmer":

> Heaven only knows the story of the lives that the gray old New England farmhouses have sheltered and hidden away from curious eyes as best they might. Stranger dramas than have ever been written belong to the dull-looking, quiet homes, that have seen generation after generation live and die. On the well-worn boards of these provincial theatres the great plays of life, the comedies and tragedies, with their lovers and conspirators and clowns; their Juliets and Ophelias, Shylocks and King Lears, are acted over and over and over again.

In this statement Miss Jewett invokes Shakespeare for duple use. She allots her own emphasis (*"All* the world's a stage") to his metaphor, and implies a comparable, if less spectacular accomplishment in characterization by laureates of narrower compass. What she wishes to call attention to, of course, is the presence of the universal in the particular and our tendency to disregard it in any but exotic guises. The slow pace and unruffled exteriors of her denizens, their reticence and inarticulateness, easily persuade strangers that no significant events or emotions punctuate their lives. Honest chroniclers of country life are therefore likely to be dismissed as arrant dabblers. "People talk about dwelling upon trivialities and commonplaces of life," she writes Mrs. Fields, "but a master writer gives everything weight, and makes you feel the distinction and importance of it."[4] And she buttresses her opinion with the assertion that our thoughts are as much engrossed by the wavering gait of Madame Bovary as they are by the woes of Hamlet.

One must be prepared, then, for much of the minuscule in Sarah Orne Jewett's transcriptions of Maine life. With patient elaboration she peoples her chosen stage with a cast of common folk moving through inexorable cycles of birth, work, and death with the dignity of figures cut in an ancient frieze. Faithful to her father's admonition that she set down people and things "just as they are," she attempts no dramatic aggrandizements of their hopes and fears, joys and sorrows. When all is said, she has brought into being a construct as peculiarly her own as Hardy's Wessex, Mrs. Gaskell's Cranford, or Faulkner's Yoknapatawpha.

I *The Place*

Although Miss Jewett sets some of her stories in large cities, in the South, and in Ireland, none of these come up to her best standards of work. In any case, these settings are extraneous to rural Maine and are not considered in the following compendious landscape—the country of the pointed firs she so lovingly records in her most cogent writings.

More prevalent than any other is the mood of withdrawal which seems to exude from the very soil, as though the region, sensible of its out-of-dateness, wants nothing to do with modern life. Loyalty to the traditions of ancestors is high in the credo of natives, whose principal aspiration is to make "old houses and boats and clothes last as long as possible."[5] They live acquiescently in strait circumstances which have prevailed since the days of the great decline. But they tend—especially the vocal old captains—to speak glowingly of the triumphs of a past they knew. Captain Sands carries on a continual panegyric about Deephaven's loftier days; Captain Witherspoon hankers after "an old-fashioned house an' an old-style vessel; there was some plan an' reason to 'em;" and Captain Littlepage, while appearing momentarily to criticize the hallowed vocation of sailing the seas, concludes with the proud affirmation: "But it made men of those who followed it."

The supreme physical fact of Miss Jewett's world is indeed the sea. Whether along shore or inland, one is incessantly bound to the sight or the sound or the influence of it. Over the inhabitants it exerts a spell undiminished throughout their lifetime. Not long after her arrival in Deephaven, Helen Denis perceives the extent of its power and attraction. "I should have imagined that the sea would become very commonplace to men whose business was carried on in boats, and who spent night after night and day after day from their boyhood on the water; but that is a mistake. They have an awe of the sea and its mysteries, and of what it hides away from us."

Standing on a short rise in this "lovely, lonely country," Miss Jewett offers breathtaking glimpses of majestic circles of pointed firs, stony beaches, green shores of tiny islands, lighthouses, and blue skies meeting on far horizons with silver-colored seas. Turning, she limns the less-inviting vista of dusky forests, stump-studded hills, swampy lowlands, and unkempt fields criss-crossed by the footpaths of successive generations. A cornucopia of flowers, shrubs, herbs, and grasses spills over the land, tempting the senses with fragrance and the mellifluous witchery of their names: chicory, larkspur, mullein, whiteweed. Of trees the most prominent are cherry, elm, the firs and spruces. The air is active with thrush, crow, heron, and gull, while in the underbrush scamper furtive small animals. No noise, no hurry disconcerts the regal procession of the seasons.

The obstreperous railroad nudges some of the larger villages and towns, where houses of older residents show signs of service and new factories bring new stores in their wake. Miss Jewett dwells less on these than upon the smaller coast and farm communities. Since the land does not yield enough to live on, the better homes are those with some attachment to the former bounty of the sea. They are more likely to be in good repair and to sport bright evidence of pewter or lace acquired in the high days of foreign trade. The view seaward, however, tells the nearer story of decline and contraction. With symbolic timeliness, sandbars are sealing off the mouths of harbors as disabled brigs and schooners go slowly to pieces by the wharves. The planking on many of these wharves has rotted away, leaving only skeletal reminders thrusting upward through mud and low water. Useless dories and wherries dot the beaches. Fish-houses, once centers of business and now final resting places for rusty anchors and discarded lobster pots, are "ready to fall down in despair."

Inland the prospect is gloomier. The grand mansions of the departed gentry have been converted to modern usage or stand as ghost-ridden relics. The trig little village houses of well-to-do spinsters or widows are decidedly outnumbered by neglected, dun farmhouses, with rows of warped outbuildings tilted this way or that. Where there is life, one is overcome by signs of primitive housekeeping and creeping squalor.

The following scene, encountered repeatedly in the back country, becomes for Miss Jewett a functional metaphor of current degradation: a deserted farmhouse kneeling behind broken gates in a field overrun by long, faded grass, its roof caved in, window panes rattling in the lightest breeze, padlock knocking against the door, hop-vine winding indiscriminately across its face and sides. Sometimes there is no house, merely the half-obscured doorstep, a crumbled chimney, and a sunken oblong, once a cellar, is choked with weeds and swarming with black ants. By infinitesimal degrees the original woodlands recapture the cleared acres. But Miss Jewett does not concede victory unconditionally in this long altercation between man and nature. "Poor land, this is!" says Mrs. Todd in "The Queen's Twin." "I've known three good hard-workin' families that come here full o' hope an' pride and tried to make something o' this farm, but it beat 'em all."

II *The People*

This dogged surge of spirit which gradually succumbs to the limitations of flesh is in fact the outstanding attribute of the men and women who inhabit Sarah Jewett's little world. The exhilaration of ocean conquest has given way to almost stoic resignation. Meager subsistence from fishing, farming, and the patronage of summer visitors is the best that they can hope for. This dwindling downward from competence to poverty has put a stamp of repressive hardness on the souls of natives who go about their daily rounds with a curious quietude, as though knowingly guilty of a huge defection yet unwilling to accept the blame for themselves. They have pride, a quirky sense of humor, and relish for their slow-paced, self-possessed lives. They seem to be waiting, perhaps for renascence, calmly imbibing wisdom from the boundless vitality of the sea and the unbroken rotation of the seasons.

Old people predominate. Because Miss Jewett revered the aged as trustees of a past she loved, and because the youth of Maine migrated to greener pastures, young adults seldom play large roles in the small communal dramas. Polly Finch, who is an instrument for the preservation of her parents, and Nancy Gale of "The Life of Nancy" are notable exceptions. Love is never passionate and courtships are most often duels of wits won by crafty, mature women. When marriages occur, they almost always come in the winter of time, as in the case of William and Esther (*The Country of the Pointed Firs*). Outside of her stories written expressly for children (for these are another area of consideration), children are practically nonexistent. Those who figure with any prominence—as Georgie West in "A Bit of Shore Life" or little Sylvia of "A White Heron"—are somber or preternaturally old.

Men are distinctly secondary in Miss Jewett's overwhelmingly female world. Not many have the sagacity of country-doctor Leslie, the solidity of marsh-islander Israel Owen, or the unadulterated goodness of David Berry. Omitting some of the resourceful fishermen, personalities run to weakness, deception, and shiftlessness. In marriage ("Marsh Rosemary") and out ("A Village Shop"), they show no disinclination to be maintained by wife or sister. The best of the boys, like Elisha in "By the Morning Boat," escape to broader fronts of experience. Those who remain take up careers of futile garrulity (the beached sea captains), of senile regression (Dan'el Gunn in "An Autumn Holiday" and Elijah Tilley in *The Country of the Pointed Firs*), or of gratuitous cruelty (the "king" of Folly Island).

By one means or another—marriage, inheritance, subtlety, utter helplessness, or force of character—women determine the shape and color of life in this subdued domain. Widows and spinsters are in the majority. Their families long dead, they have become accustomed to living alone, are frightfully neat, and follow undeviating schedules of daily activity. They show inordinate curiosity about the slightest occurrence in the parish, ready to lay praise or blame upon friend or foe. They treasure their last rusty black satin "going-out" dresses and other sentimental remnants from the splendid shipping days.

A recurring type is the versatile, self-reliant female who will not be deterred by circumstance. A host of these sanguine women comes immediately to mind: Mrs. Kew, Hannah West, Nan Prince, Polly Finch, Ann Floyd, Eliza Peck, Esther Jaffrey, Mercy Bascom, Hannah Pinkham, Ann Ball, Betsey Lane, Maria Durrant, Mrs. Peter Lunn, Almira Todd, Mrs. Blackett, Esther Hight, Cynthy Dallett, Mrs. Sullivan, *et aliae*.[6] From copious reserves of courage or tenacity they draw the spiritual energy needed to carry them through their comfortless situations. Many are women who turn out to be better "men" than their menfolk.

Miss Jewett usually equips her more feminine or inept elderly ladies with compatible and complementary sisters. They have lived so long together in self-contained seclusion that there is little to distinguish between one and the other. "The Dulham Ladies," "Mary and Martha," "The Town Poor," and "In Dark New England Days" are constructed upon this condition. The effect in each instance is to intensify the pathos by compounding the misery.

The influence of the old gentry is to be felt in their relics or seen in their descendants. An air of past magnificence still hovers around Miss Brandon's imposing white house in Deephaven, as it does about delicate, demented Miss Chauncey. Horatia Dane in "A Lost Lover" and the protagonist of "Miss Sydney's Flowers" are versions in a less decorous day of the traditional great lady. In different ways, Dr. Leslie and Miss Anna Prince infuse *A Country Doctor* with gentility foreign to the latest generation, while Esther Jaffrey ("A Village Shop") seems momently about to don ancestral vestments.

The indigenous eccentrics who comprise the stock and trade of most local colorists are not absent from Miss Jewett's bailiwick. But she and the community exhibit protective tolerance and a certain amount of fondness for their oddities. Long familiarity with the comic, pathetic, or tragic history behind these aberrations has stripped them of the novelty they present to newcomers. The country of the pointed firs is dotted with uniques like the bird woman in "A Little Traveler," the hallucinated father in "The Landscape Chamber," the intransigent "king" of Folly Island, and Abby Martin, the *soi-disant* twin of Queen Victoria. The narrator of *The Country of the Pointed Firs*, attuned to the nuances of regional sympathy, notices the "peculiarities of character" in Captain Littlepage but refrains from interrupting his fantastic memoir. She has come to realize that the strength of the group consists in a sustaining flow of relation from the highest to the lowest, which excludes the possibility of any individual being permanently isolated.

The natives speak a language which has the color and texture of the soil they walk upon. They refer to *ellum trees* or to *rosbry time;* they feel *grum* or *peart;* they own a *power of china* or *suffer a master sight of trouble;* they differentiate between new and fresh lobsters; they make *a touse* about things and exclaim, *"Good King Agrippy"* about people who don't *spudge up.* They seem to mind less if a man is *all talk and no cider* than if he is *wamblecropped.*

A common store of superstitions and folk practices adds more resource to their solidarity. The three old women at the Thacher cottage (*A Country Doctor*) discuss the queer "doin's of sperits," and the Dunnet villagers bandy rumors about Indian specters on Shell-Heap Island (*The Country of the Pointed Firs*). The overweening presence of death is endorsed in a variety of localized observances. Death is personified in the mysterious Gray Man; portents are transmitted through the sounds of death-ticks in the wall or the sight of trees withering near a house; and bees are notified of death in a family by black crepe hung over the hives. Meddling with foxglove will bring upon one the wrath of fairies. Codfish swallowing stones forecast a storm, and chickadees perched upon a window ledge anticipate the arrival of a stranger. Four-leaf clovers inserted in the shoe will attract lovers by the score.

The analogous features of landscape, the tendency of people to fall into classifiable types (although invincibly individual), the social and religious accord, the kindred language and folkways in Miss Jewett's world—all these coalesce to give it a look of relative homogeneity. To enhance this effect, she uses several suggestive devices. Names of places recur in different sketches and stories: York, Dulham, Longport. So do cognomens: Dunning, Downs, Prince, West, Crowe, Pinkham, Chellis, and others. Characters reappear in other stories or volumes: Kate Lancaster and Helen Denis of *Deephaven* are heard of in "Good Luck: A Girl's Story," and Father Miles of "The Luck of the Bogans" in "A Little Captive Maid." To create vertical as well as horizontal continuity, Miss Jewett depicts the changeless resemblance of the faces in Deephaven church to those of their colonial ancestors.

With the uninsistent firmness of an assured artist, Sarah Jewett draws a small but vital portrait of a special place and people, more profoundly authentic than any in her own time and one excelled by few in any time.

III   *The Themes*

From earliest maturity Miss Jewett was convinced that "the real drama of life" was to be found in "a dull little country village." In the city "only the glaring virtues and strident vices" became apparent. "The delicate cadences are lost in the blare of heavy tones."[7] With this limiting principle as guide, she treats such themes as are best illustrated by her typical dull village. The themes themselves are broad and fairly simple; it is her implementation of them that is subtle. Since themes and implementations of specific works are examined at some length in subsequent chapters, the concepts and doctrines she considered most meaningful in the daily life of her sequestered society are only briefly coordinated here.

(1) *Decline of New England.* The fabric of her work is shot through with this rueful topic, which amounts to a mood as well as a theme. In the sketches Miss Jewett speaks directly from primary observation of persons and scenes that corroborate her point. She also resorts to expository statement in her narratives, but in these she is apt to utilize symbols of nature, situation, character, or action to fortify her intent. She presents multifaced permutations of this theme, from ancestor worship to migration to spiritual decay in such stories as "A Village Shop," "By the Morning Boat," "The Failure of David Berry," "Little French Mary," and "The Landscape Chamber." The reign of poverty and apathy in a region once virile and self-reliant is the main spur to Miss Jewett's creative impulse. It drives her into an almost tragic revelation of the effects of defeat, defeat necessary to a people for proper recognition of their essential selves.

(2) *Past versus Present.* Miss Jewett's ingrained preference for the older generation and her distrust of the emerging techno-logical culture lead her into numerous contrasts between the genteel values imbedded in her memory and the more raucous current ones. "From a Mournful Villager" voices her bias exten-sively and explicitly. Occasionally, however, a tincture of doubt shadows her nostalgia. In "The Dulham Ladies," for instance, she indulges in more than ordinary irony while reciting the stately annals of the past.

She also comments briskly on the comparative worth of youth and age, a focused correlative of the larger theme. The laurels go most frequently to the aged, but Miss Jewett is not averse to bestowing excellence upon the young ("An Only Son"). Sometimes the reader must balance accounts for himself, as in "The Hiltons' Holiday" or "A Landless Farmer."

(3) *Nature.* Physical nature, whether beneficent or ill-favored, serves as more than backdrop in Miss Jewett's stories and sketches. She engages it actively in symbol and analogy (techniques discussed below), and she also employs it themat-ically to grasp its psychic impress upon man.

In its salutary aspect nature imparts to country people a sense of the strength and purpose of the world about them. They listen to the words of sea and field and forest, absorb the meanings of the universal creative power, and accept instincts as truth. Because they trust their primal instincts so completely, they enjoy a truly Wordsworthian sympathy with nature. It becomes for them the final reality. On the reverse side of the shield, nature lies in wait for man with persistent hostility as he ineffectually tries to subdue its vigor. Worsting him in the lonely places, nature irresistibly covers up the traces of his fatal struggle.

Miss Jewett's interest in the relationship between man and nature develops into a thesis concerning the influence of climate upon character. She attributes the flinty disposition of Mainers to "the spirit of the North," the cold weather which discourages the kind of carefree pleasure possible in Italy or along the sunny banks of the Nile. In "Andrew's Fortune" she equates life in frigid New England to "a stunted bloom" existing in spite of the destructive weather. She also notes the changes undergone by colonists from old England after they have lived for a spell in the new climate. And she sees idle sons of south Ireland stimulated into unwonted activity by the east winds and "our own keen air." This transfusion of the physical with ethical and spiritual properties is another mark of her superiority over purely local colorists.

(4) *Heredity*. In *The Tory Lover*, Major Tilly Haggens declares bluffly, "'Tis all settled by our antecedents," but Sarah Jewett herself is not satisfied with such dogmatic simplicity. Her graph of the power of heritable qualities issues from *A Country Doctor* and several of the short stories. Nan Prince is the exemplar of Miss Jewett's belief that materials accumulate through several generations and then appear in a child who is the heir of all the family wit, beauty, and common sense—precisely as one might inherit the worldly wealth of his ancestry. Up to seven or eight years of age children are simply clusters of inherited traits; then they begin to assert their own individuality. Some, to be sure, find themselves with no usable force to bring into play, but Miss Jewett maintains that human beings have the capacity to overcome their worst inheritances and climb to their best possibilities.

Miss Jewett makes no noteworthy departures from conventional nineteenth-century theory in applying the effects of environment and heredity to her New England folk. Although she sometimes instructs the reader in a vexing platform tone, the resultant characterizations are discreet and credible.

(5) *Country versus City.* Contrasts between these diverse ways of life infiltrate all of Miss Jewett's important work. In her mind this polarity is allied with her theme of the decline of New England and her antithetical view of past and present. The wane of rural areas is a direct consequence of economic innovations in the cities. The country represents a treasury of all that is good in the past; the city, all that is dreadful in the present.

With few reservations, Miss Jewett assigns virtue to the country and vice to the city. Four of her novels hymn the supremacy of country over city, and all her stories dealing with business contain dour comments on prevailing ethics. The country is natural, easy, simple, and dignified; the city, artificial, agitated, prejudiced, and money-mad. Country women are reserved and self-sufficient; city women, volatile and helpless. Adeline Prince, who goes from country to city, bows to temptation and is demolished. Sylvia, who goes from city to country, rises above temptation and is exalted. Irish and French peasants who settle in cities deteriorate from the ravages of drink, bad drainage, and factory work. The city practices heartless duplicities upon naïve countryfolk: the Misses Dobin in "The Dulham Ladies" and the Pinkhams in "Fame's Little Day." New Yorkers, as a species, look "crafty."

Mrs. Peet ("Going to Shrewsbury") drives home Miss Jewett's point once and for all with a sprightly, scornful localism: "Town folks has got the upper hand o' country folks, but with all their work an' pride they can't make a dandelion."

(6) *Religion.* Although Miss Jewett turned out several analogues of biblical stories, such as "Mary and Martha" and *An Empty Purse,* and utilized quotations from the Bible in numerous others, she does not insist upon the dogmas of any particular theology. Her religious attitudes, often put in the words or thoughts of her characters, take on the semblance of a tetra-towered edifice. Visible in her rather vague but comforting religiosity are a conventional Christian God, a romantic pantheism in nature, a bio-ethical ascendency, and a concept of directive fate.

The black icicles of Calvinism prevalent in other sections of New England do not overhang Sarah Jewett's Maine communities. An amenable faith which goes back to Galilean tenets and makes no parade of evangelical ardor guides most of her solemnly decent people through conditions conducive to a more puritanical outlook. The general view is that God has been good, sparing of trials and liberal with blessings. He plans and orders all, grants to each a special role and the capacity to fulfill it. Nan Prince (*A Country Doctor*) is confident that outside her own preferences and choices, a wise purpose has been at work with her and for her. After long indecision she perceives that God has revealed His orders to her at last. As a matter of observable fact, God's providence is timely and widespread. At moments of dire need—as in "A Late Supper," "The Night Before Thanksgiving," "A Business Man"—He may be relied upon to produce a *deus ex machina.*

The ethics and the ideals which brace this simple scheme are equally simple. Love, hope, and charity compose the central pillars. The relationship of the three old poorhouse inmates in "The Flight of Betsey Lane" is more than mere companionship in misery; it sustains the last shreds of spirit in a material world that has come to the end of the line. Father Ryan's unflinching love for the reprobate in "Between Mass and Vespers" brings about a miracle of rehabilitation. The spontaneous optimism and fortitude of Nancy Gale are in full accord with Christian principles; so is the self-sacrificing zeal of Debby Gaines at Christmas time.

In *Deephaven* Kate Lancaster opines that "God himself [is] in the world, and . . . we may read the thoughts that He writes for us in the book of Nature." This Emersonian dictum Miss Jewett expands into a cyclical concept of life in nature that has some likeness to Whitman's in "Song of Myself." Life and matter are inseparable, and God the Creator puts into use again and again the life that is withdrawn. In "River Driftwood" Miss Jewett speculates about an evolutionary rise in the scale of continuous existence; from grass to beef to human being seems a not illogical process to her. Here, as in her manifold nature–man correlations, she aligns herself squarely with nineteenth-century American transcendental doctrine: the indissoluble interconnection of God, man, and nature.

Another supramundane idea pervading the novels and short stories is that of fate as an ordering force. Frequently it is indistinguishable from the personal hand of God or it allows the intervention of human self-reliance; on the whole, it complicates and confounds Miss Jewett's preceding views on nature and a Christian deity. Fate is an inexplicable power that abrogates decision and moves men in directions outside their will ("The Only Rose"). The predestined, mechanistic plan of their lives is never really broken, never susceptible to pure accident. John Frankfort is sure that he has drifted "under some pilotage that was beyond himself" into the quiet haven of Folly Island; Tom Aldis meditates upon "the curious insistence of fate which made him responsible for something in the life of Nancy and brought him back to her neighborhood."

But free will is not ineffective against this seemingly unalterable organization. Although the mad father in "The Landscape Chamber" mutters that men may fight but are doomed at the last, Miss Peck achieves her promotion through self-help despite a deterministic conspiracy of events. God's providential manipulations may also obstruct the aims of fate, as the fortunate outcome of Miss Becky's pilgrimage indicates.

While not entirely negating freedom of will nor questioning the primacy of God, Miss Jewett confers upon fate a function of considerable prestige. At least three of her protagonists feel that the motive powers within them are lying in abeyance, awaiting the "orders" of fate to set them going: Nan Prince in *A Country Doctor*, Dick Dale in *A Marsh Island*, and pert Betty Leicester.

(7) *Duality of Human Nature*. Superficially or intensely, comically or seriously, Miss Jewett continually suggests the inscrutability of even the most artless personalities. She probes conflicting elements in the human psyche; she demonstrates in myriad ways the gulf that divides appearance and reality. On a predominantly physical level she uses the device of assumed identity in "The Taking of Captain Ball" and of duple identity in "The Two Browns" to objectify the urge to transmute one's recognized role in society. Miss Eliza Peck analyzes her problems by candidly discussing them with her other self—a manner which calls to mind *Strange Interlude*. Miss Jewett examines the variance between internal actualities and external expressions of love in "A Lost Lover," "The Quest of Mr. Teaby," and "Miss Esther's Guest." Surprisingly dissimilar temperaments are masked under placid or formidable miens in "Fair Day" and "Miss Sydney's Flowers." "An Only Son" and "A New Parishioner" deal with differences between what is believed and what is true of a person. In "A White Heron," "A Second Spring," and "A Neighbor's Landmark," Miss Jewett registers poignant struggles be-

tween assertive factors within individual consciences. Although simplicity is a byword with her, Sarah Jewett is under no illusion that it applies to the devious interplay of heart and mind, or to the slightest relationships between her ostensibly impassive folk.

(8) *Social Usefulness.* Especially in *A Country Doctor,* but also in a number of the short stories, runs this strain: "the secret of happiness in this world is not only to be useful but to be forever elevating one's uses." Dr. Leslie's iterated "I want you to be all the use you can" influences Nan Prince's determination to become a doctor, to serve society rather than self. Miss Jewett approaches the Puritan ideal in "Miss Becky's Pilgrimage" when she paraphrases the Johnsonian maxim that life is to be endured, not enjoyed: "We are in this world for the sake of discipline, and not enjoyment." Then she wonders whether the Reverend Mr. Parsons takes disappointment in love "as an indication that he would be more useful as a single man." In salient cases of selfishness or degradation she berates the shameful waste of useful, God-given talents.

Miss Jewett's sympathy with the ethos of her native region was, by her own account, congenital. Her uncommon comprehension of the landscape and people was gained during childhood and adolescence. Thus, when she wrote about what she knew best, it conveyed no sensation of surprise or revelation; she was only serenely sharing an integral part of herself. Charles Miner Thompson has put this most poetically:

> I always think of her as of one who, hearing New England accused of being a bleak land without beauty, passes confidently over the snow, and by the gray rock, and past the dark fir tree, to a southern bank, and there, brushing away the decayed leaves, triumphantly shows to the fault-finder a spray of the trailing arbutus. And I should like, for my own part, to add this: that the fragrant, retiring, exquisite flower, which I think she would say is the symbol of New England virtue, is the symbol also of her own modest and delightful art.[8]

CHAPTER 3

Pastel in a Metal Frame

MANNER not only encompasses *style,* an elusive term involving personal tone and turn of presentation, but also *technique,* the strategies of characterization, structure, and treatment which make for effective literary composition.

Sarah Orne Jewett's first book demonstrates that she had a style distinctly her own despite traces of preceding writers. "What the books are, she herself preëminently was."[1] Simple country people and activities were inerrably the materials that suited her disposition and talent. This she recognized instinctively. "It is rather discouraging to find I lose my best manner by studying hard and growing older and wiser!"[2] she complains to one of her early editors. Playing the sedulous ape to no particular masters, she arrived at uniqueness of manner by mining and refining her own emerging tendencies.

From the start her sketches and stories shine with a special quality, flawed here and there by uncertain or ungainly experiments. Steadily she eliminates the immaturities and blemishes until in 1896 she touches the summit of her artistry in *The Country of the Pointed Firs.* Matthiessen is extreme in his verdict that without style her material would be too slight to attract a second glance, but it is undeniable that style has sustained her work through periods which fed on meat rawer than she served.

I The Pathetic and the Comic

Tone is the bedrock of Miss Jewett's continuing appeal. William Dean Howells told her: "Your voice is like a thrush's in the din of all the literary noises that stun us so."[3] It is indeed so hushed and unhurried that her tidings run the risk of going unheard. Her feminine gentility which permeates every attitude and utterance results in an inflection that Edward Garnett calls "exquisite spiritual gravity." She looks across the lost days and re-creates them tenderly. Uncritical nostalgia fogs her vision but galvanizes her memory. "The old houses look at each other as if they said, 'Good heavens! the things that we remember!' "[4] So she sings an elegy not necessarily melancholic for a rich and piquant past more alive to her than the present. And with much of her work she imparts a suggestion of "old-fashioned romance put into modern terms," a quality she ascribes to Anne Thackeray's "Cinderella."

Voluntarily addicted to graciousness, affability, and resignation, Miss Jewett never develops a competence to deal with the tragedies of compulsion and repression which mark the blockaded lives of women in, for instance, "The King of Folly Island," "The Landscape Chamber," "The Town Poor," and "In Dark New England Days." Sympathy for their predicaments evokes only expansive pathos which, by firm exercise of good taste and a hearty sense of humor, usually stops short of sentimentality.

Pathos is implicit in Miss Jewett's landscape of blighted farms and disintegrating seaports, and the inhabitants assimilate distress as a kind of ineluctable legacy. Primary situations that induce compassion are rife: the loneliness of the poorhouse inmates in "The Flight of Betsey Lane," the grinding poverty of Mrs. Robb in "The Night Before Thanksgiving," the helplessness of the old sisters in "Miss Sydney's Flowers," and the tribulations of the aged in "The Failure of David Berry." Miss Jewett draws what commiseration she can in her accounts of the orphaned child in "A Little Traveler" and of the bereaved parents in *A Marsh Island.*

Probing more deeply into the personal dynamics of pathos, she discloses the pangs of women who mistakenly believe they are loved by men (Ann in "Marsh Rosemary"), women whose lives have been blasted by a luckless affair (Joanna in *The Country of the Pointed Firs*), and women who have missed the warmth of romantic love (Esther in "A Village Shop"). Miss Jewett dramatizes the irony of self-delusion plangently in the case of the Queen's twin, pleasantly in "A Late Supper," and rather wryly in "The Dulham Ladies." Shifting her attention to the defects of community character, she defines the pathos of short-lived gratitude in "Decoration Day." With consummate resource, she prevents pity from turning maudlin through an unexpected deliverance or a bracing touch of comedy.

Miss Jewett's humor comes in many forms and is preponderantly low-keyed. Only her satire (noted below) and several events expressed in the hyperbolic western style (*e.g.*, "Miss Debby's Neighbors") diverge from the tenor of friendliness. Comedy is more abundant than one would estimate until he begins classifying its varieties. Miss Jewett exploits the humor of character through a legion of amusing eccentrics, through the rustic drolleries of Jim Fales in *A Marsh Island*, through the guarded byplay between the widow Tobin and Jefferson Briley in "A Winter Courtship."

She makes ready use of stock comical situations: the careless amplifications of gossip in "The News from Petersham," the provincial naïveté in "The Luck of the Bogans," the manipulated identities in "The Two Browns" and "The Taking of Captain Ball," the O. Henry-like twists in "The Only Rose" and "All My Sad Captains," and the benign skirmish in "The Quest of Mr. Teaby." Miss Jewett appreciates the farce possibilities in "Tom's Husband" and "The Passing of Sister Barsett," and she unearths anecdotal riches of the region in "The Courting of Sister Wisby" and "The Coon Dog." In the verbal vein, she exudes mock horror and maidenly whimsies, puns in her titles, and brings to full fruition the quaint or racy native parlance—"worse than a kitten in a fit"; "I declare if you ain't the same old sixpence"; "I ain't goin' snappin' through torment in a hemlock coffin."

This is the merest sampling of the kinds of good-natured humor Miss Jewett indulges. Continually she propounds the quality which keeps her people from succumbing to their demoralizing plight—a primal sense of humor compounded of courage and self-depreciation, evinced in laconic or jocose terms. Therein she displays sympathy and allegiance. But she is capable of sharper, detached assessments. Ironies and satire interlace her novels and short stories.

In *Deephaven* she delivers a cutting female jab at kindly Mrs. Kew, whose bedroom—hung in evidently poor taste with likenesses of relatives and friends—"was partly devoted to the fine arts." Oddly, she again attacks a subject usually sacrosanct to her when she twits the Jaffrey family tree in "A Village Shop." Love invites several of her barbs, for she unfairly equates hapless old Ann Floyd with "Juliet on her balcony," and she swipes at the extravagant self-consciousness of young love in "The Mate of the Daylight." With clinical precision Miss Jewett exposes the disparity between illusion and reality in "The Dulham Ladies," and portrays with almost vicious delight the confrontation of two social dragons, Mrs. Flagg and Mrs. Timms. Neighborliness, the backbone of lonely New England countryfolk, receives questionable respect in "Bold Words at the Bridge," as does the ministry in "Martha's Lady."

Two major tones, then—the pathetic and the comic—reign in Miss Jewett's work. When pathos seems dangerously about to prevail, it is effectively counterbalanced by an infusion of comedy. And when humor of the too comfortably homey type threatens to overwhelm, Miss Jewett brings matters around with a caustic observation or two. She is at best when she qualitatively blends pathos and humor, creating out of them a superb image of the recessive land and its valorous inhabitants. The multiplying misfortunes of Catherine Spring in "A Late Supper" and the "unusual malady" of Miss Bond in "The Flight of Betsey Lane" provide serviceable examples in a long list of such situations and characters.

II *Felicities of Style*

Miss Jewett's outstanding virtues of expression are simplicity, clarity, and economy. Her prose flows effortlessly, uncluttered by studied phrases or tortured figures, and gives off a subdued radiance which is best described in Louise Imogen Guiney's words, "Simplicity, with glory."[5] Numerous passages in *Deephaven* illustrate the fluency, the impeccable diction, and the lack of complexity and affectation which mark her artistry from its beginnings. As she matures, the essential features remain the same but the bloom takes on a deeper hue and texture.

Her faultless rhythms and consistent lucidity raise comparisons with a variegated company. Some critics see in Miss Jewett's simplicity and control a mild accord with the classical Greek temper. Others associate her feelings for nature and her accurate epithets with Dorothy Wordsworth's, her half-poetic studies of background and character with Howells', her presentation of quaint atmosphere and personalities with Hawthorne's. For flavor and finesse she is mentioned with Chekhov and De Maupassant.

Gallic compactness and clarity are indeed prominent in her style. These are most often attributed to the influence of Flaubert, whose "two wonderful bits" of literary maxim she kept pinned on the little drawers at the back of her writing desk as constant reminders:

Ecrire la vie ordinaire comme on écrit l'histoire.

Ce n'est pas de faire rire—mais d'agir a la façon de la nature, c'est à dire de faire rêver.[6]

Although she read and frequently discussed Flaubert, it is more likely that she gravitated toward him because of mutual aims rather than that she consciously modeled her style upon his.

The felicity of her style is most manifest in her management of native idiom. She extracts the peculiarities of speech from the earth of their origin, turns up their roots with some of the soil still clinging, yet preserves unharmed their vibrant connection with life. So artful is her artlessness that Lowell once congratulated her for being "discreet in dialect, using it for flavor but not, as is the wont of many, so oppressively as to suggest garlic."[7] Her restraint is rare in the local-color literature of her day. She is, in fact, in a class of her own.

III *Creating Characters*

Characterization presented some serious problems to Sarah Jewett until she began to concentrate almost exclusively upon the region and people she truly knew. In such early stories as "Mr. Bruce" (1869), lack of intimacy with urban settings and sophisticated characters misleads her into bald superficialities. Her thin, typical men and women fail to come to life in the course of action. *Deephaven* suffers from Helen's penchant for supplying data about natives when they do not stand still long enough for a full portrait. Miss Jewett's trouble up to now is technical, not cognitive. Through each of her succeeding volumes she eradicates flaws and comes closer to the superlative portrayals for which she has the capacity. However, some awkwardness persists. Mr. and Mrs. Owen, Temperance and Dan, characterize themselves in *A Marsh Island*, but many of the others emerge through the author's omniscience. The collections *A White Heron* and *Strangers and Wayfarers* represent Miss Jewett at her best in characterization. She exposes the depths of personality simply but with indelible effect by depending less than ever upon incident and more and more upon the individual's own instincts and utterances. Thereafter—excepting the unconscionably wooden

The Tory Lover—her exposition of character is usually as unobtrusive as the flow of her prose rhythms.

She devises no esoteric means of character revelation; she merely bends conventional usages to her special proclivity. In the role of author as narrator she divulges valuable insights into motivation by falling into extended ruminations about characters and their habits. This she does in the first person in "A Bit of Shore Life"; or, in the third person, she outlines with short, broad strokes the odious nature of John Mander in "The Night Before Thanksgiving." Increasingly, as time goes by, she permits characters to reveal themselves through thoughts, speech, and interrelationships; but at any moment she may intrude a gratuitous opinion. She exemplifies this manner in crude but full coloration in *A Country Doctor;* she refines it fittingly to her purpose in later works.

The ironies of self-revelation appeal strongly to Miss Jewett. What people say and how they say it become prime indicators of character. In *Deephaven,* Helen tells us about Kate but unintendingly unveils quite as much about herself in the process. Frequently two persons are joined in a protracted dialogue ("A Winter Courtship") with the same result. Sometimes there is a third—in what may be called a triologue—to provoke sparks of temperament from a more complicated interchange, palpably as in "Decoration Day" or abstrusely as in "Miss Tempy's Watchers." Mercy Bascom releases useful clues by talking to herself in "Fair Day," but hers is a mere habit of loneliness in comparison to Miss Eliza Peck's self-colloquy, which brings to light a dual personality.

Miss Jewett also uses the comments and reactions of a chorus of knowing villagers to invigorate portraits of both central figures and community ("A Second Spring"). Even more often she introduces an outlander who brings fresh viewpoints to bear upon attributes in danger of being overlooked by inured natives ("The Quest of Mr. Teaby"). And she makes capital of two devices recollective of Hawthorne in "The Minister's Black Veil" and *The Scarlet Letter:* character unfolded through a procession of encounters—the spirited lad's leave-taking of his family and friends in "By the Morning Boat"; and character implied by externalities—one's looks, clothes, habitation—as in "The Gray Man" and "Between Mass and Vespers."

But Miss Jewett is not uniformly successful in characterization. At the outset of her career, the editors of the *Atlantic Monthly* singled out the weaknesses in her presentation of young men. And while her greatest strength lies in minutely realistic reproductions of aging farmer- and fisher-folk, she tends to ignore their worst shortcomings or to pass them off with a smile. Some notable exceptions have already been mentioned, but in large part Miss Jewett prefers not to explore the labyrinths of psychological ugliness. Men who grossly disfigure the lives of their daughters, for instance, either have died ("In Dark New England Days") or are plainly crazy ("The Landscape Chamber"). But she is aware of what she is shunning; in *A Country Doctor* she has Dr. Ferris expatiate upon the "intense, self-centered, smouldering volcanoes of humanity" in New England which have no match the world over.

In her best vein Miss Jewett expounds the drama of individuals at once harried and sustained by discomforts of flesh and pride of spirit. She embroils the basic elements of kindness, self-denial, faith, humor, hope, and resignation in miniature internal conflicts and shows their shaping effects upon lonely, undemonstrative souls. Through their protective mists of solitude and silence, Miss Jewett discerns contradictory reactions of terror and exultation: they realize the implications of aloneness but are fiercely comforted by intimations that their wills are free. Respecting both the terror and the exultation, Miss Jewett usually allows them to proceed in directions of their own choosing; she is loath to deflect them from the prosperity or disaster they wilfully invite.

IV *Man and Nature*

Sarah Jewett's people are endowed with such ingenuous sensitivity to the moods and meanings of nature that they appear absolutely at one with landscape and weather, their natural habitat. In a letter to Sarah Wyman Whitman she likens the figures she sees in a Maine potato field to Millet's immemorial French peasants.[8] This is a pertinent association; she shares fully that artist's genius for suggesting the poetic and mysterious correlation of man and the soil. It is equally difficult to separate her rustics from the land as it is to distinguish Millet's gleaners in their rapt intercourse with the shorn earth.

Through consistent use of analogy and symbol, Miss Jewett reasserts the reality of this primeval interdependence between man and nature. She may link them in workaday similes: one of her heroines is as bright as a rose, another has the freshness and toughness of a cedar tree, while hepaticas remind her of some people, "very dismal blue, with cold hands and faces." She enlarges the range slightly when she opines that, like the moon, many of us always have one side hidden and turned away; and when Mercy Bascom ("Fair Day") enters the house she once lived in "like some shell-fish finding its own old shell again and settling comfortably into the convolutions."

In "River Driftwood" she proffers the biography of a river as illustration of her theories about the influence of heredity and environment upon man. In a similar connection, she describes the stifling of love's pangs as "the contentment of winter rather than that of summer," and avows that Polly Finch has made "as good a summer's growth as anything on her farm." The tall, thin spruce at Haydon's door in "A Second Spring" bears a likeness to the solitary old man himself, and Almira Todd is sure that there are as many "strayaway" folks as there are plants of that variety.

Miss Jewett does not hesitate to commit the pathetic fallacy when she wishes to emphasize the oneness of man and nature. Bayberry bushes wake up and conclude it is not yet spring; John Packer swears that he "ain't goin' to have them trees murdered"; and during an autumn walk Miss Jewett "stopped by each of the stray apple-trees that came in my way, to make friends with it, or to ask after its health, if it were an old friend."

In *A Country Doctor* she develops a transcendental equation worthy of Emerson. The child Nan, sitting in an old summer-house, is exhilarated by the coincidence of the parishioners' singing and the loud solo of a robin in a cherry tree. Other situations embracing natural creatures in symbolic mimicry of human activity occur in "Miss Esther's Guest" (dialogue of the golden robin and the old bullfinch), and "By the Morning Boat" (Elisha freeing the woodchuck). Maine flora is also put to symbolic function. The twisted lilac in "A New Parishioner" acts as a warning to Miss Dunn of Stroud's crookedness, the barberry bush teaches Polly Finch a lesson in circumspection, and the elusive wild rose in *A Marsh Island* seems a sad presentiment to Dan Lester.

Nature as a beneficent instrumentality is the base of at least two of the short stories. The peril of extinction which threatens the white heron is enough to swing Sylvia, product of a manufacturing town, into perfect alignment with nature. Miss Sydney's beautiful flowers eventually convert her misgivings into a philanthropic view of the human race—and also dissuade a young man from evil plans. These intimations of divinity at work in nature Miss Jewett substantiates explicitly in "A Winter Drive": "If a man or a tree has it in him to grow, who can say what will hinder him. . . . I believe that it is more than a likeness between the physical natures, there is something deeper than that."

Striving for some absolute that eclipses mere resemblance between man and nature, she discovers in "An October Ride" that "I am only a part of one great existence which is called nature. The life in me is a bit of all life, and where I am happiest is where I find that which is next of kin to me, in friends, or trees, or hills, or seas, or beside a flower." Her submergence of personality in the immensity of nature approaches the mystic ecology of Thoreau at Walden Pond. In "A Dunnet Shepherdess" Miss Jewett assumes a mood of total receptivity: "If there is one way above another of getting so close to nature that one simply is a piece of nature, following a primeval instinct with perfect self-forgetfulness . . . it is to take the course of a shady trout brook." And this quintessential rapport can be established only through the most intimate reciprocal involvement: "Whatever man's hands have handled, and his thoughts have centered in, gives something back to man, and becomes charged with his transferred life, and brought into relationship. The great pines could remember all the Packers" ("A Neighbor's Landmark"). One understands why Mike Bogan carefully wraps a square of turf in his best Sunday handkerchief before leaving Ireland for the uncertain new world across the ocean.

These are some of the reasons why Miss Jewett descries attributes of the highest order in her apparently wasted people. They walk through fire hand in hand, sharing eternal perceptions, unappalled by the dross of their immediate circumstances. Theirs is the strength of Antaeus. No one smiles when Miss Jewett imputes a bearing of grave, archaic royalty to her shabby men and women or proposes that Antigone and Almira Todd are sisters under the skin. Courage born of a secret knowledge has elevated them above the generality. Miss Jewett's greatest asset is that she sees this without distortion and relays it without affectation.

V *Prototypes*

She may have arrived at this totality of apperception through the bookish process she described in a letter to a child: "And then the people in books are apt to make us understand 'real' people better, and to know why they do things, and so we learn to have sympathy and patience and enthusiasm for those we live with. . . . It is just the same way that a beautiful picture makes us quicker to see the same things in a landscape."[9] Certainly she creates no people out of whole cloth, nor does she present improbable syntheses of country "characters," the staple of inferior local colorists. She confides the origination of three of her fictive personages to one of her chroniclers:

> They were actual discoveries. In one house lived "Aunt Tempy" and watching the quiet way in which she passed on the small blessings of life, the kindly smile, the gentle word, the helping hand, the gift from her own small store to some one who had even less, I was unconsciously evolving the "Aunt Tempy" whose passing would leave so wide and deep a void. In another poor little home was the self-abnegating milliner, longing for a wider opportunity to make some one else happy, and in a more imposing dwelling the rich lady of the little community, who would have enjoyed being liberal, had not some dead hand of her ancestors stretched out through the generations and held her back from the indulgence of generous impulses. So there were "Aunt Tempy and her Watchers" ["Miss Tempy's Watchers"] ready to hand.[10]

A spate of references in Miss Jewett's letters certifies this as the principal channel through which authentic individuals reached the pages of her books. Around the beaches and fish-houses of Wells she observed not only the idiosyncratic widower who appears as Elijah Tilley in *The Country of the Pointed Firs* but the marvelously self-sufficient youngster who becomes Georgie West in "A Bit of Shore Life." She recounts the details of several visits to frail old gentlewomen whose forbearing counterparts inhabit so many of her stories. She identifies the peddler upon whom she modeled Mr. Teaby. Doris Owen and Dan Lester of *A Marsh Island,* Ann Floyd of "Marsh Rosemary," and Miss Chauncey of *Deephaven* are similarly accredited as real persons. Doughty Mrs. Todd seems to have been derived from a neighbor of Miss Jewett during a vacation in Martinsville.

These and others of their kind she conceived as prototypes. They recur throughout her works with variations appropriate to setting and situation. Mrs. Todd, for example, first comes to view in rudimentary form as The Widow Jim in *Deephaven*, later as Mrs. Goodsoe in "The Courting of Sister Wisby." Kitty Tennant, Kate Lancaster, Bessie Thorne, and Mary Leslie comprise the inquisitive, euphoric young girl who sheds vitality upon everyone she meets. Dan'el Gunn forecasts Elijah Tilley, just as Danny does William Blackett. The daring young man who fares into broader vistas of experience, and sometimes returns to the scenes of his childhood, is represented diversely by callow Elisha, Andrew Phillips, Daniel Lewis, Parker Jenkins, Johnny Harris, the Honorable Joseph K. Laneway, and Henry Stroud.[11] The lovable tyrant of the kitchen, a compound of Juliet's nurse and George Eliot's Mrs. Poyser, crops up in a number of guises: Melissa in "A Lost Lover," Marilla in *A Country Doctor*, Hetty Downs in "The Dulham Ladies," Temperance Kipp in *A Marsh Island*, and Mrs. Powder in "Law Lane." By judicious distribution Miss Jewett embodies these repetitive similitudes of type without descending to stereotype.

VI   *A Romantic Realist*

Miss Jewett never mustered her thoughts about literary theory and practice into convenient, compact expression as did Poe in "The Philosophy of Composition" and "The Poetic Principle." A system must be assumed from her collected work and from scattered recipes she provides for inquiring novices. She seems of two minds on this score, even within the bounds of a single letter. To her friend Rose Lamb she advocates study of "work that the best judges have called good" to "see *why* it is good," while insisting that "it is the personal contribution that makes true value in any form of art."[12] The stories and essays show innumerable signs of another tug of war between realistic and romantic treatment of material.

She vacillates less in the more abstract area of the creative process. With the reasonable differences that her temperament and circumstances would make, Miss Jewett's explanation of the way an idea rises in the mind and is then transformed into literary art has antecedence in Plato's *Ion* and Wordsworth's Preface to *Lyrical Ballads*. In Plato's version, poets are without volition, producing beautiful poems through the autonomous activity of inspiration. They speak many noble words, but "we who hear them may know them to be speaking not of themselves . . . but that God himself is the speaker." They are powerless to create until they attain a state of utter acceptance of God's desire. In tones of Christian awe rather than pagan ardor Miss Jewett accedes to metaphysical direction and possession. To a critic she writes: "We come to our work by strange paths—we hardly know how."[13] And to an editor: "I don't wish to ignore such a great gift as this, God has given me. I have not the slightest conceit on account of it—indeed I believe it frightens me more than it pleases me."[14] Like Emerson's Michelangelo, she builded better than she knew. Instead of an invincible formula for the construction of a tale, there is "that *something which does itself*" and "stories that write themselves in spite of you."

After the divine seizure, an indeterminate period of maturation sets in which is not unlike Wordsworth's "emotion recollected in tranquillity."

> Good heavens! what a wonderful kind of chemistry it is that evolves all the details of a story and writes them presently in one flash of time! For two weeks I have been noticing a certain string of things and having hints of character, etc., and day before yesterday the plan of the story comes into my mind, and in half an hour I have put all the little words and ways into their places and can read it off to myself like print. Who does it? for I grow more and more sure that I don't![15]

To Willa Cather she puts it in slightly different words—"the thing that teases the mind over and over for years, and at last gets itself put down rightly on paper."[16] Not invention, but experience, sympathy, and imagination are the powerful adjuncts of inspiration. In proper time the immediate vivid impression finds its way into a happy combination of images and an ideal form.

This inherent romanticism makes itself felt in Miss Jewett's treatment of the familiar materials surrounding her. Pattee opines that she went about equipped with a camera, but Matthiessen thinks she abstained from lifeless photography. A balanced conclusion must take into account that on occasion she transcribes the grubby aspects of environment with unblinking accuracy, but that on the whole—to recruit Wordsworth's Preface again—she throws "a certain coloring" of her own imagination over it. Upon granitic surfaces she spreads a poetic spell not entirely idyllic; under the lovely sheath the harsh configurations are implicitly visible. The over-all effect is that of a pastel framed in metal. If hers is not always a starkly true report of life, it is a convincing rendition of a very real part of it.

Miss Jewett is essentially a prim and incipient realist whose roots remained fixed in a depleted romanticism. She speaks of her mode as "imaginative realism," and she persistently refuses to be governed by uncompromising fact. Howe recalls the following conversation between her and Henry James:

> "It is foolish to ask, I know," he said, "but were you in just such a place as you describe in the 'Pointed Firs'?" "No," she said, "not precisely; the book was chiefly written before I visited the locality itself." "And such an island?" he continued. "Not exactly," she said again. "Ah, I thought so," he said musingly.[17]

In letters and in the 1877 Preface to *Deephaven* she makes similar disclaimers.

The first rank of Continental realists (Flaubert, Zola, Turgenev) was soon joined by a strong contingent of like-minded British novelists—Thomas Hardy, George Moore, and George Gissing. As had been the case since the seventeenth century, the new English emphasis was soon adopted with enthusiasm in America. Before the 1890's had run their course, Miss Jewett could have read such morose examples of the new realism as Hamlin Garland's *Main-Travelled Roads* and *Prairie Folks,* Frank Norris' *Moran of the Lady Letty* and *McTeague,* Stephen Crane's *Maggie: A Girl of the Streets,* to say nothing of the grim vignettes of her less fastidious New England counterpart, Mary E. Wilkins Freeman. These changes in the literary ambiance did not escape her notice. She makes what use she can of their disquieting revelations and, as before, denies the implication of specific influence: "I remember Mr. Howells asking me with great interest long ago when I had written the story of a 'Landless Farmer,' if I knew Turguenieff's 'Lear of the Steppe'; but I did not then or for a few years after."[18]

As a matter of fact, if the stamp of any single author is distinguishable in the writings of Sarah Orne Jewett, it is that of

William Dean Howells. Their acquaintance and her homage began when she was not yet twenty and he accepted one of her earliest stories. From close readings of his creative and critical works, she learned that, for one, "Mr. Howells . . . frowns upon the romantic." She learned many another lesson, as even a tenuous comparison will show: they both favor plots without complexity or manipulation; they both write of the commonplace, eschewing aristocratic milieu and the cult of the hero; they both use dialect and localisms in the service of character; they both temper the winds of realism with romance and humor, and veer from the bleaker shores of tragedy; they both defend the continuing alliance of art and morality. That Miss Jewett learned her lessons well is to be gathered from the accolade Howells bestowed upon "the exquisitely realistic art of Miss Jewett."

VII *Point of View*

Miss Jewett's artistic techniques are admittedly sedate and leave her open to the accusation of monotony. But for the plasticity and diversity with which she handles point of view, the volume of reproof would be greater. She of course utilizes methods perfected over the ages but she lends them a peculiarly personal quality which surrenders nothing to convention or expediency. Her insights are products of experience simultaneously felt and objectified. She tries to explain this to Willa Cather, advising the younger writer to immerse herself in her backgrounds but, at the same time, not to stand in the middle of them.

Sarah Jewett knew that "dull old Wells is a first-rate place to find stories in." She also knew that, if she wished to rescue them from the doldrums and vivify their integral values, she would have to present them from angles interesting to a removed, presumably unappreciative audience. The task before her was to reconstruct a moribund situation in vital terms yet not to misrepresent the mood or the pace, to reconcile the conflicting prodigies of character—what people are, what they believe they are, and what they appear to others. The widening gap between the world of Dunnet Landing and the world of the machine made for more than ordinary difficulties. Her victory did not come easily.

Her first experiments with point of view are strained and

cumbersome. Too often the story-within-a-story sags of its own weight because, no matter who takes over as narrator, Miss Jewett perceptibly usurps the role. The narrator of *Deephaven* frequently addresses the reader in a way that hampers rather than promotes intimacy. By her second volume Miss Jewett is handling the sustained, familiar third-person omniscient level with fair competence. However, her practice of stepping into or aside from the story line to admonish characters or readers continues to plague her work well into its best years.

Book by book, she gains in versatility and suppleness, letting narrators speak from their own vantage points and in their own accents. For variety and verisimilitude she shifts from person to person within a single story, generally opening with two in conversation and eventually introducing others. The eyes and voice of the community are effectively infused in "The Dulham Ladies" and "The Taking of Captain Ball." Notably in "A White Heron," she enters and leaves the consciousness of the protagonist to attain multiplication of view.

When she wants most acutely to bring out both the apparent and obscure elements in her backward precincts, she operates through impressible outsiders and knowing insiders. The former come in coats of many colors. Kate Lancaster and Helen Denis—young, naïve, breathless—supply freshness of perception and excitement of discovery no longer available to Deephaven natives. John Frankfort, a man matured by the iron disciplines of business, actuates a wave of sympathy for the long-slighted daughter of the "king" of Folly Island. The out-of-region summer visitors who narrate "A Bit of Shore Life" and *The Country of the Pointed Firs* combine acuity of vision with a predisposition for the place, people, and mores. Miss Jewett contrives numerous variants of this device and complicates it further by contrasts between city–country ("The Life of Nancy"), North–South ("A War Debt"), and foreign–American ("A Little Captive Maid").

To plumb the deepest undercurrents of Maine character and manners, Miss Jewett resorts mostly to her beloved spinsters and widows. Through the gnarled shapes of their past, their present conduct and remarks, she materializes the tenacious spirit of a continuing civilization. (The sad captains are less useful in this function, for they have lost touch with the current world and reflect only the irretrievable splendor of a dead day.) The Widow Jim, who knows everyone's secrets and can attend

anyone's illness, is Deephaven's organic spokesman. Mrs. Goodsoe, the "simple-hearted soul made out of the old-fashioned
country dust," is admirably the same in "The Courting of Sister
Wisby." The redoubtable gossipmonger of *A Country Doctor,*
Mrs. Meeker, is coexistently a terror and a treasure. Ezra Allen
("A Landless Farmer") and Jonas Phipps ("A New Parishioner"), male representatives of the type, are drawn with only
slightly less efficacy.

Miss Jewett sometimes compounds these perspectives, and
adds dramatic tension, by uniting the outsider and insider points
of view in one person: the native who leaves Maine and returns.
The hearts of Senator Laneway ("A Native of Winby") and
Rebecca Parsons ("Miss Becky's Pilgrimage"), to name only two,
overflow with comparisons between then and now and there
and here.

Despite these seemingly deliberate applications of technique,
Miss Jewett's short stories are not patterned after the French
pièce bien faite, nor do her novels conform to theories of sequen-
tial development and crisis. Formalistic control might have aug-
mented the strength and appeal of her books but, as is so often
repeated, she was writing to please herself. Although she con-
cedes that "there must be a solid foundation of drill and accuracy
and certainty and *justesse* of touch,"[19] she wrote "impulsively—
very fast and without much plan,"[20] ever fearful that too much
dedication to method would leave its inevitable smell of the lamp
on her work. She prefers "that something which is so much better
than art," the purely private quality that Howells fitly ascribed
to her stories. "They used to be as long as yardsticks, they are
now as long as spools, and they will soon be the size of old-
fashioned peppermints, and have neither beginning or end, but
shape and flavor may still be left them."[21]

Any discussion of Miss Jewett's techniques should include at
least partial quotation of Lowell's tribute, written for a publisher's untitled circular:

> Miss Jewett has wisely chosen to work within narrow limita-
> tions, but these are such only as are implied in an artistic nature
> and a cheerful compliance with it. She has thus learned a dis-
> creet use of her material and to fill the space allotted without
> overcrowding it either with scenery or figures. Her work is nar-
> row in compass, like that of a gem-cutter, but there is always

room for artistic completeness and breadth of treatment which are what she aims at and attains. . . . They are artists in the best sense, who could make small means suffice for great ends. . . . Miss Jewett . . . possesses and practises this precious art.[22]

For reasons of his own, Matthiessen places Sarah Orne Jewett with Emily Dickinson in the highest echelon of female American authors. If so exalted a position is warranted, credit must also go to the insistent individuality, the copious heart, the innate understanding, and the unruffled sensibility that informs every line of her mature writings.

CHAPTER 4

Down the White Rose Road

THE ESSAY, fashioned in the eighteenth century into a vehicle for urbane wit and social edification by Addison and Steele, was turned to more personal account by English masters of the form in the generation preceding Sarah Jewett's. Lamb, Hazlitt, and Leigh Hunt opened its windows and poured into it melodious diction, humor verging on whimsy, and the world's potpourri of subject matter. Thackeray and Stevenson continued in the tradition and insured its popularity as a major literary genre through the Victorian epoch.

In tone, outlines, and commixture of topics Miss Jewett's sketches call up all of these predecessors. But the parallel nearest home is Nathaniel Hawthorne, whose "soft miracles"—particularly "Sights From a Steeple," "Footprints on the Sea-shore," and "The Toll-Gatherer's Day"—are classics in this vein. Miss Jewett is less detached, but otherwise the same kind of spectator: wise and amused and sad and charitable about the pains and pleasures of common folk in common pursuits, she assays and accepts the daily round that is man's portion. The essence of Miss Jewett's finest quality emanates from these sketches, "light as smoke or wisps of sea-fog, charged with the odours of mint, wild roses and balsam."[1]

After some five years of publishing verses and short stories predominantly for children, Miss Jewett submitted "The Shore House" to the editors of the *Atlantic Monthly*. This proved to be the first in a series of pleasing familiar essays about the shoreline and backland areas of Maine. At the outset Howells censured her for not making more of it, and held the script without taking action. Cognizant of her technical and temperamental limitations, she put her case squarely to Horace E. Scudder: "I am certain I could not write one of the usual magazine stories. If the editors will take the sketchy kind and people like to read them, is not it as well to do that and do it successfully as to make hopeless efforts to achieve something in another line which runs much higher?"[2] Her logic must have prevailed, for the sketch came out in September, 1873, and was collected later, with strategic alterations, as the first two chapters of *Deephaven*.

The *Atlantic Monthly* subsequently offered its readers most of the sketches now available in her volumes of selected works. Some were rejected and did not come to light until she included them in one of her collections. By 1889 her periodicals market for this specialized material seems to have have dried up. Only the regional sketches which were to comprise *The Country of the Pointed Firs,* and several sequels, appeared thereafter. (The thirty-seven chapters of *Deephaven* and *The Country of the Pointed Firs* embrace the characteristics of the sketch but they are discussed under the broader category of novel, the putative form into which Miss Jewett cast them.)

Her first efforts in the field of the familiar essay were frankly experimental; she felt she could have made them better if they could have been longer. They radiate a quiet, callow charm, are lucid in thought and expression, but lack substance and the pulse of vitality. Two elements noticeable in the beginning and persistent to the end are minimal incident and pliable organization. In time, the force of a maturer personality and a surer instinct shone through the pale tincture which—even so truculent a critic as Ludwig Lewisohn agrees—is not the least faded after so many years. With "A Bit of Shore Life" in 1879, Miss Jewett demonstrates that she has come into full mastery of this mode. Her best independent sketches, published in 1880-81, are included in *Country By-Ways*.

Paramount in these sketches is her manner—a mingling of the serenity of a saint and the assurance of a chatelaine, at once sympathetic and self-possessed. It has a trace of the *noblesse oblige* that Pattee suggests,[3] but it is more a conjointure of ingenuous love and the necessary objectivity of the artist. These sketches divulge the pith and tenor of her affections. She walks or rides the bypaths of her chosen domain; records sensual impressions of farm and seascape, the dress and talk of the folk; probes the secret springs of their existence; and reflects upon their history, traditions, ideals, and current condition. These data, obvious or opaque, she presents through a special overlay of romanticized realism. Diffused or not, they comprise an irrefutable guide to the conduct and meaning of life in nineteenth-century rural Maine.

I   *The Sketches*

"A Bit of Shore Life," for example, affords glimpses into quite a bit more than merely shore life. While spending some idle days by the sea, Miss Jewett is invited to a farm six miles inland. On the way, she stops to take in an auction of household effects. After her visit, she completes the circuit by returning to the seashore. Through this picaresque sortie she discloses shore and farm and the country between, as well as a cross-section of inhabitants in daily procedure.

Miss Jewett displays a marvelous eye for detail and a genius for making friends. Her first conquest is twelve-year-old Georgie West, the shy, precociously mature son of a widowed fisherman. Georgie is small and strong, with a dry brown face and horny hands. He remains silent unless prodded, then replies sententiously. He has no cronies his own age, and is almost belligerently diligent about any task set him. Love of the sea is the first reality of his life; he fishes alone in his boat until long after nightfall. His ideal is to emulate the "rest of the men" in their heartbreaking devotion to their ships. In his oilskin suit, cut down from one of his father's, he symbolizes the continuing tradition of the Maine fisherman.

Georgie's aunts, Hannah and Cynthia West, are two of Miss Jewett's frequently encountered spinsters. Hannah is tall and large, with a forceful, unequivocal manner, "what the country people call a master smart woman, or a regular driver." She has been a schoolteacher briefly and has moved in orbits wider than their back-country farm. Her education and experience, coupled with native ability and resourcefulness ("I'm the one who has faculty," she tells the narrator), give her unflinching self-confidence. She controls her environment and her weaker sister.

Cynthia West is "one of the faded-looking country-women who have a hard time." Overshadowed by her sturdy sister, she feels of little use or consequence. She apologetically confides her girlhood dreams of perhaps keeping school, of perhaps living in Boston, of perhaps seeing something of the world. But she stays on, pathetically dependent, knowing she cannot live out of sight of the woods.

Old Mrs. Wallis and her high-handed but solicitous son provide a second contrast. John Wallis has made a fortune in Boston and has now come to take his mother back with him. On the morning Miss Jewett arrives, the dingy homestead is bustling with neighbors who have come for the auction. Wallis insists that every last article be sold or given away; he wants no shabby keepsakes around his newly built and furnished home in the city. Mrs. Wallis has lived all her hard-bitten life in this wretched home and has become so attached to everything in it that the thought of selling even a cracked and mended bowl is repugnant to her. She flutters about helplessly in a web of ambivalence; she is eager to please her successful son yet distraught about having to leave the house whose doors have been worn smooth by the touch of her hands.

The Wests and the Wallises point up Miss Jewett's ceaseless concern over the fate of Maine. Just as Cynthia West reflects the debilitated vigor of the new generation and Hannah the indomitable spirit of the old, so Mrs. Wallis reveres rural mementoes of the past while her son prefers urban values of the present. Here, as in many other places, Miss Jewett balances the strengths and weaknesses of old and new, country and city, through significant antithetical figures. Mrs. Wallis makes a comment on the disparity between youth and age which sums up the import of the piece: "Every thing looks fair to him, and he thinks he can have the world just as he wants it; but *I* know it's a world o' change,—a world o' change and loss."

Mood is set by Miss Jewett's frequent diversionary asides, some pious, some philosophical, but all based on sharp observation. She falls into a long rumination about the sadness and loneliness that afflicts people (especially elderly women) who live on farms on the outskirts of villages and about the morbidity of interest they show in the pettiest occurrence. She discovers no real merriment in their odd, rough jokes but enjoys their quaint humor and occasional flashes of wit. She recalls Whittier's poem when she notices black cloth over some beehives. Her account of the impromptu tea prepared by Hannah—biscuit, hot gingerbread, lobster, two kinds of preserves, honey, and pie—has the savor of pure Down East. But the initial tableau of "good-natured fishermen, who were lazy and busy by turns, who waited for the wind to change, and waited for the tide to turn, and waited for the fish to bite, and were always ready to gossip about the weather, and the fish, and the wonderful events that had befallen them and their friends" rings a note of indulgent love which is audible throughout. Miss Jewett's quiet certitude about character, scene, and custom impinges long after one puts this sketch down.

The title "River Driftwood" (1881) promises a miscellany and does not disappoint. Miss Jewett, cruising along the eastern branch of the Piscataqua River which separates Maine and New Hampshire, recounts the history of its importance to the Berwicks and its decline as a waterway with the advent of railroads. She dispenses incidental data about the ships and shipyards once pertaining to the river, the fine houses in its vicinity, the eminent personages who knew its waters, and the traditions that bind all of these together. She injects family reminiscences; tales of fun and adventure along the river banks, of famous clerics in nearby towns; and local anecdotes and superstitions—not unlike Cotton Mather in his wondrous mélange, *Magnalia Christi Americana.*

Miss Jewett's expression, though hardly as crabbed as the Puritan divine's, misses its characteristic felicity. The style is (for her) elevated and overrun with literary and classical allusions, particularly in the early sections. She invokes several ponderous whimsicalities about cruising to Europe in a small boat, understanding a pimpernel's language, schoolrooms for swordfish and swallows, and supper with a muskrat. A curiously self-conscious monologue lacking her usual warmth, it improves as it progresses, becoming expansive in descriptive passages of nature —"the sparkling river and the blue sky, the wide green shores and the trees, and the great gray house . . . the lilacs in bloom, and no noise or hurry,—a quiet place."

Whereas in "A Bit of Shore Life" Miss Jewett swings in a wide circle to collect her impressions, in "River Driftwood" she floats down a medial river, stopping at one bank or another to watch this or that phenomenon within sight or hearing. Meanwhile her mind darts swiftly up sundry tributaries of thought, returning to and departing from the mainstream in a pattern of manifold radiation. The river provides an axis which keeps the topics from tumbling into an indiscriminate heap.

Contemplation of numerous analogies between man and nature leads Miss Jewett to postulate an ascending order of existence in terms that recall Emerson's epigraph to *Nature*. Her concept derives from the venerable metaphor of a Chain of Being. In her case it does not end with man but, romantically, presumes an additional link nearer perfection—the angel. Quite unromantically, however, she welds it to Darwin's doctrine of the survival of the fittest:

> When one thinks of whole races of small creatures like the mussels which are the natural and proper food of others, it seems an awful fact and necessity of nature; perhaps, however, no more awful than our natural death appears to us. . . . A death that preserves and elevates our identity is much more consoling and satisfactory. . . . Who can say, however, that our death may not be simply a link in the chain? One thing is made the prey of another. In some way our present state ministers to the higher condition to which we are coming. The grass is made somehow from the ground, and presently that is turned into beef, and that goes to make part of a human being. We are not certain what an angel may be; but the life in us now will be necessary to the making of one by and by.

This line of discourse leads her to "the transmigration of souls and other puzzling subjects," so she hurries back to the safer haven of "my river."

One other primary thesis in "River Driftwood" is the superiority of the past over the present. Miss Jewett sighs over the disappearing old wharves whose rotted piles are cenotaphs of better days, and she deplores the cheaper satisfactions of contemporary living—standard houses, the railroads, the telegraph. She resurrects from local memory the story of the physician who pretended to great riches but was found at death to be destitute. Madam Hovey, his widow, is a Jewett archetype—the *grande dame* in reduced circumstances—who can be met again in Miss Chauncey, Lady Ferry, and Mistress Sydenham. Madam Hovey, serenely magnificent, delivers no recriminations over her fallen estate. She lives alone, dresses well, and is rigorous in all rules of etiquette. Fantasy invades her lonely activities, and poverty and old age unnerve her. But she makes no sign in public—she is "a high-bred lady." Such people as Madam Hovey are the backbone of Sarah Jewett's belief in the nobility of the past: "The Guard could die, but it never surrendered, and the old prestige was kept bravely." This shibboleth supports Miss Jewett's lifetime regret that she was born too late.

The main road in "A Winter Drive" (1881) is equivalent to the river in the preceding sketch. Miss Jewett rides over and around a succession of paths which conduce a spate of physical and metaphysical observations. The presence of contemporaries—her horse and driver, the clam-man, teamsters and farmers—infects the air with liveliness and checks her proneness to fall into absorption with the past.

The cynosure of this essay is trees. She cites George Morris' appeal to the woodman and would doubtlessly have incorporated Joyce Kilmer had his distichs been available then. She applies Ruskin's pathetic fallacy liberally—most trees are like most people—and makes much of the hamadryad myth. She notes that it may be more than coincidence and chance which cause a tree to fade and die when the man or woman with whom it has been associated dies. These and other curious homologues dispose her to the ancient doctrine of hylozoism, "the theory of the soul of the world, of a life residing in nature, and that all matter lives."

These intrinsic likenesses in the natural order move her to speculate about the concomitance of a moral order. She hesitates to assert that the higher animals are morally responsible but finds it impossible not to believe that trees have thought and purpose, for "they show traits of character which one is forced to call good and evil." At what level of existence self-consciousness first appears she is not prepared to say. She is confident, however, that it is present in the higher orders of vegetable life and in the lower orders of animals.

Digressions of this kind are in accord with the logic of ramification which determines her course during the long drive. Moreover, they do not disturb the superbly unnoticeable rhythms of her writing, particularly when delineating nature, whose frigid bareness she can appreciate as fondly as its summer pulchritude. Her banter about the "invisible telegraph"—which spreads news faster down main thoroughfares and along crossroads than a man on a horse—somewhat dissipates the gloom around women seasonally incarcerated in lonely farmhouses.

Miss Jewett had no luck trying to convince the editor of *Harper's* that "An October Ride" (1881) was drawn intact from life.[4] She eventually gave up hope of periodical publication and unveiled it to the public for the first time in *Country By-Ways*. This sketch retains the radial scheme of straying off and trending back to the highway. There is more to the structure this time, however: two focal points from which emerge the basic tone and theme. Miss Jewett's reflective ramblings over the country-side take her to the ruins of a farm and to an abandoned parson-age. At both these shrines (for such they turn out to be) she invokes the ghosts of former inhabitants, who are, to all intents, delegates of the spirit of the past.

After some leisurely remarks about her horse and the York woodlands, she heads for "this farm of mine," which now consists of a very large cellar grown over with grass. She stands in the spell of the quiet, tree-hidden place, remembering the En-chanted Palace and the Sleeping Beauty in the Wood. She has only heard about the last owner of the house—a famous old spinner long dead—but the woman is now vividly real to her. She visualizes the old lady living alone, sitting by herself in a square pew in church, dressed in quaint fashion, and brooding sadly over the passing of her old companions. How fearless she must have been to have stayed year in, year out, in such a place as this! To all dead pioneers, Sarah Jewett pays this loving tribute.

From here she proceeds by devious routes to a parsonage now deserted and beginning to fall to pieces, but once the abode of a renowned minister. After giving the blackened brass knocker a ceremonious rap, she unfastens the bolt and starts her explora-tion of the denuded rooms. Although the minister's books have been taken away, she feels a close communion through the many stories she has heard about him. She pictures him dozing in his armchair before the fireplace, a brown old book laid on his knee. She gathers some scattered boards, lights a fire, then sits in a salvaged chair until the day wanes, relishing her expe-rience to the full. On leaving, she wonders who made the first fire there, and she hopes she has made the last. This perpetua-tion ritual represents her inviolate connection with an extin-guished way of life. She cannot bear to have the hearth dese-crated by others for the mere sake of comfort, and she accepts herself dotingly as the last in her generation to tend the sacred flame.

In both these episodes, Sarah Jewett calls up the past with a nostalgia achieved at second hand. Knowing neither of the pro-tagonists, she re-creates them through artifacts and hearsay. The atmosphere is one of withdrawal from the realities of the day. Nothing alive affects her except the horse Sheila, whose moods and movements function like the knocking at Macbeth's gate to restore the bemused rider to the problems of the present.

The two reveries evince a partiality for the aged which manifested itself in her early childhood. In the solemn self-sufficiency of the old spinner and the learned gentility of the old minister Miss Jewett personifies qualities she considers most estimable in the New England tradition. She hankers passionately after them, yet her native shrewdness and honesty do not permit total capitulation to illusion. At one point in the parsonage she muses on the irony of relative values: "And it is very odd to think that these iconoclastic and unpleasant new times of ours will, a little later, be called old times, and that the children, when they are elderly people, will sigh to have them back again."

In "An October Ride" Miss Jewett strongly reaffirms the amity between man and nature but she also dwells on a less hospitable facet in the relationship—nature's inveterate opposition to man's attempts to cultivate the land or to set up permanent monuments to his skill. As she looks at the void which was once a farm, she ponders the inevitable defeat of man, a martyr to "the law of existence in its succession of growth and flourishing and failure and decay." These cogitations open the way to her profoundest pronouncement of faith. Man can at best mould the world's accessible forces to his use; he cannot create new forces. "We grow spiritually, until we grasp some new great truth of God; but it was always true, and waited for us until we came. . '. . But it is only God who can plan and order it all."

From her sketches, then, one perceives Miss Jewett's religion as an odd amalgam of elements drawn from experience and simple trust. She is as responsive to the living principles of nature as she is to the biblical piety of Victorian New England. With the heedless ease of innocence, she embraces components of a mystical affinity with nature which is transcendentalism, a scaled biological destiny which is Darwinism, and a belief in the absolute sovereignty of an anthropomorphic God which is Christian dogma. (The power of fate which moves men's lives autocratically—a power she often confuses with God's omnipotence—is a fourth principle, operating primarily in her fiction.) The anomaly never seriously troubles her. If she has any doubts or conflicts, they are minor and creedal. God is unquestionably the fountain from which all life flows.

"From a Mournful Villager" (1881) is Miss Jewett's most intensive inquiry into the grammar of local mores and social traditions. The subject is broached without preamble: the approaching extinction of front yards in New England and of the village character and civilization with which they are associated. With so forthright a start, one might thereafter expect continuous survey of a theme so absorbing to Miss Jewett. But, as before, her mind wanders to and from related areas, utilizing the front yards as a locus of reassembly—"But to go back to the little front yards." She strays into autobiography in the latter portion of the essay but preserves a loose unity through recall of the front yards and repeated reference to gardens and flowers.

Miss Jewett's opinion as to what happened to "the old-fashioned provincial society" carries some of the implications of Frederick Jackson Turner's classic paper on "The Significance of the Frontier in American History," delivered some twelve years later. Turner denies that American institutions were a mere continuation of European beginnings. He sees the advance westward as a successive movement away from the influences of Europe. The frontier promoted a new composite American who was formed by his adaptation to and mastery of the primitive conditions he met. Coarseness and acquisitiveness became dominant traits—Jacksonian rather than Jeffersonian democracy, the ideal.

"For many years," writes Miss Jewett, "New England was simply a bit of Old England transplanted." Although she sees many examples of English-oriented customs surviving in the eastern parts of New England, she grants that they are distinctly in the minority. "The representative United States citizen will be, or already is, a Westerner, and his instincts and ways of looking at things have certain characteristics of their own which are steadily growing more noticeable." In a reverse wave, the new culture of the West returns and washes away remaining traces of colonial traditions. She dramatizes the situation by transferring "one of our own elderly ladies" to the midst of provincial English society where she would be quite at home; then to the west of the Hudson where she would be a stranger and a foreigner.

After a diplomatic curtsy to the present, she promptly turns her back on its so-called advantages and deliberates upon the ways of gentler days. There was less communication between villages then. People stayed within their own horizons, addressing themselves to their own land, their own neighbors, and their own affairs. A traveler was a curiosity. She verifies the defect of this closed society but commends its depth of interests and feelings. Now and again she thrusts at the immorality of cities, a temptation she can seldom resist.

She occupies herself next with the necessity of honoring the "grand prestige and dignity" of elderly people, comparing them to wines of fine vintage. She refers with feministic pride to the altered position of women since the fight for equality began. Once they were confined to the house and a prim corner of garden; nowadays the whole world is their front yard. And she speaks another word for the outmoded virtues of reserve and separateness, taking the same position as Robert Frost's succinct neighbor: "We Americans had better build more fences than take any away from our lives."

She pokes some well-bred fun at Puritanism for its proscription of dancing and whist, then veers into a topic closer to her heart—visiting. House-to-house social calling is no longer the important function it used to be, a change she attributes to new-fangled habits of travel encouraged by railroads. (This obsolete village program of visiting she weaves into the fabric of her fiction, notably "The Guests of Mrs. Timms" and "Aunt Cynthy Dallett," just as she transforms her divagations about trees in "A Winter Drive" to drama in "A Neighbor's Landmark.") After a slanted compliment to "modern progress and success," the mournful villager concludes with a far-from-mournful account of her childhood which contains the often cited, "I was first cousin to a caterpillar . . . I was own sister to a giddy-minded bobolink," as well as frolic peeks into her playroom, her pleasures and peccadilloes.

In "The Confession of a House-Breaker" (1884) Miss Jewett returns to the matter of man's integral kinship with nature. The content is admirably sustained by the style, which is a happy example of her undulating, undemanding, low-keyed, pleasurably pastel prose. Descriptive, reminiscent, and contemplative, it blends the best qualities of the personal essay—intimate as Lamb, picturesque as Stevenson, and (taking away his intellectuality) discursive as Hazlitt.

Barring a slight foray into the metaphysics of sleep, Miss Jewett dallies on the level of sensual perception during a walk through her garden and the village streets in a June dawn. Sleepless one night, she decides to slip out of the house and worship the advent of morning. In her solitary meanderings she arrests and reflects a swarm of impressions: a bat, the moon, flowers, birds, a sober toad, trees, a flickering lamp, a wailing child, a sleeping dog, the sky at dawn. When the cocks break the spell of dawn, she hops over the front fence and re-enters the house. As the mill bells peal, she drowses off. Thus her matutinal expedition assumes a neat cyclical shape and is rounded with a sleep. Her ramble transpires in an atmosphere of fantasy, and when she wakes in the morning she is as delighted and puzzled by it as if it were a dream. It was; and into it she had poured all her romantic fancy for the mystery and solace of nature.

In the preceding sketch Miss Jewett enjoys Hazlitt's recipe for going an outdoor journey: "liberty, perfect liberty, to think, to feel, do just as one pleases," and above all, to go it alone. In "A Little Traveler" (1884) she echoes his preference for society when indoors. The *mise en scène* is a railroad train, which she populates with a graphic agglomeration of characters: a pair of diffident newlyweds, two loquacious elderly women, a fantastic old lady with a bird cage, four or five businessmen, a stout Catholic priest, and a personable little orphan girl. Through a series of interrelations which just misses evolving into a short story, Miss Jewett reveals a gallery of saucy portraits within an edifice of mild pathos.

Miss Jewett, when she befriends the young girl on her way alone to an aunt in Boston, learns that she does not yet fully comprehend the recent death of her mother. The child's pretty manner makes itself felt as she goes about talking to other passengers. The bride weeps and holds her close, the priest blushes and is confused at her ingenuous advances, and the bird-woman is diverted by the child's pleasure in her pet. By journey's end everyone on the train has given her some small gift of fruit or candy. Even the priest, unsympathetic at first, kisses and blesses her at parting. Miss Jewett lingers tremulously at the station and is relieved to see the aunt's demonstration of instinctive love.

The ability of a child to bring out the humanity in a disparate company of indifferent adults is a hoary romantic theme which had been revived with raucous sentimentality a decade before this by Bret Harte in "The Luck of Roaring Camp." Aiming at a similar dilation of group compassion, Miss Jewett tends to the extreme of homiletic treatment. "I could not help thinking how often we are at each other's mercy as we go through this world, and how much better it would be if we were as trustful and unsuspicious as this little child," she says, envisioning an impossible prelapsarian world of no guile.

The bird-woman and the Catholic priest are salient psychological studies, but the former is more memorable. She is traveling with an extraordinary amount of luggage, odd bundles, and a bird cage holding a fat, tame robin. At home, she explains, she has twenty-three birds in all, thirteen of them canaries. And she goes on explaining—who is taking care of them while she is away, where she is going, who she will stay with, her name, et cetera, et cetera. Her readiness to confide personal details to utter strangers points up a significant paradox in so close-mouthed a region. She also underscores the indulgent attitude of the community toward eccentrics so entrenched in their peculiarities that they no longer suspect they may be queer.

One may well wonder why Miss Jewett chose to uncover altruism in a railroad train, which she ordinarily presents as an emblem of destruction or depravity. Certainly the compactness of the area and its restricted constituency recommend it as an ideal stage. Perhaps she felt that the incongruity itself might lend greater force to her unabashed message. Regardless of intent, "A Little Traveler" stands today as an excellent illustration of her major strength and weakness: incisive, suggestive, and rich characterization—and effeminate incapacity to put it to dynamic purpose.

After the fecund period of 1880-81 Miss Jewett produced no sketch of comparable quality until "The White Rose Road" in September, 1889. In the interim she enhanced her skills and reputation with two novels, a history, children's stories, verses, anecdotal narrative, social comedy, and some of her most moving short stories.

"The White Rose Road" represents total reversion to the style and concerns of the familiar essay. If the tone seems somewhat more sedate and the diction under firmer control than in the earlier pieces, there is nevertheless no loss in cordial relation with the reader. Once more Miss Jewett is out driving with John, her "master of horse." As they move seaward along this storied route of young lovers her mind roves restlessly from exposition to description, to meditation, to opinion, to anecdote, history, personalities, legends, regional data, apocrypha, and nature. She wanders in memory to Virginia on a slim trail of flowers and returns on a magic carpet of gay New England blooms.

Although her response to nature shows several fresh accretions, it remains fundamentally the same. Her first pages are a paean to the weather and the lovely June vista, but twice she regresses to a darker note—the eternal contest for supremacy between untamed nature and *homo agricola*. She notes, without partisan sentiment, that forests are pushing their outposts farther into the pastures year by year, "as if they had no idea of losing in their war with civilization and the intruding white settler." The final phrase implies a romantic concept of the noble savage not professed before. She declares Indians the kin of pine woods and the only proper figures belonging therein. Elderly people of the region regard the woods distrustfully, with "something more than a fear of losing their way." We are left to suppose that this terror is a synthesis of human guilt and "some unrecognized but malicious influence" immanent in the woods, a favored motif of Hawthorne's. Characteristically, Miss Jewett does not press the point. Thereafter, nature beams benevolently through her sporadic reflections.

The sketch is alive with people she meets or remembers as she passes their former abodes. She peers with undisguised sympathy at the placid old houses, knowing they are mere façades behind which toil and sorrow are unremitting tenants. A thin little girl busily farming her special plot arouses the rider's admiration. She can see that the soil is "backward" and that the child's labors will probably come to nothing. But the spirit in the small body is unquenchable. Before us is arrayed in miniature the morose prospects of a fine-grained folk in a barren situation.

A too easy pathos glosses the portrait of the old farmer's family. He is crippled from war wounds, and Miss Jewett cannot resist the frayed symbolism of a half-withered rose lying within his reach. His wife was chairbound for many years before her death; the two grandchildren are orphans. Excess aside, these generations represent the past and future of staunchest New England stock. The man has dignity, self-possession, and sobriety of manner; his wife never succumbs to "that malady of the spirit, a desire for ease and laziness"; the granddaughter is quick and shy; the grandson, a replica of Georgie West, is industrious and reliable. Upon the shoulders of these four rest Miss Jewett's revered traditions of courage and self-respect, which she takes pains to assure the reader are vital and perennial. The boy and girl "had learned a fashion of life from their elders, and already could lift and carry their share of the burdens of life." Their parents, the current operative generation, are significantly dead.

On the homeward stretch Miss Jewett encounters a funeral. She reports with remarkable perception its social and emotional impact on the community. Most impressive is the solemn figure of the mother of the deceased, a woman of great age and infirmity. When looking at the group, the passer-by sees only her. "She was like a presence out of the last century, tall and still erect, dark-eyed and of striking features, and a firm look not modern, but as if her mind were still set upon an earlier and simpler scheme of life. An air of dominion cloaked her finely." Upon this matriarch Miss Jewett confers the title of queen, for "Royalty is a quality, one of Nature's gifts." Lady Ferry, Mistress Sydenham, and others in Miss Jewett's canon bear this air of tragic majesty. It is, indisputably, their due heritage from a long line of unyielding forebears and their own long chronicle of sufferings and silences.

In one expanse of three miles Miss Jewett marks with sad foreboding only one house that is occupied and six ruins that had once been prosperous farmhouses. If the old farmers who wrested these homesteads from the wilderness could see them now, what would they say of the younger generation? Miss Jewett's displeasure with the present finds new targets in the factories and tanneries which are polluting clear New England streams and making good river fish scarce. She launches a brief polemic on the need for fish conservation laws, impulsively alleging that man does his best to despoil the world he lives in. But at the instant gloom seems about to envelop the atmosphere conclu-

sively, she mounts the last hill before reaching the village. From
this symbolic eminence she surveys the pleasant houses, the
green fields, sundown—and concludes that all is not lost. Man
may yet grow wiser about fish and other things. Thus, at the
last, man and nature are turned to happy account despite evident
blemishes. In Sarah Orne Jewett's world, optimism is as near
as the next hill.

In the foregoing sketches, Miss Jewett sustains an illusion of
unity through various stratagems of movement—cyclical, radial,
the ramble afoot, the countryside ride—or through the confines
of a moving railroad train. Thus, technically, she evades the
effect of Carlyle's "beautiful bags of duckshot held together by
canvas." But the true cohesive in her sketches is tonal, a quality which resists communication in critical terms. Willa Cather
tried to distill it in an impressionistic simile: "like bringing the
tenderest of early spring flowers from the deep wood into the
hot light of summer noon without bruising its petals."[5] But there
are also verve and levity and rare common sense in Miss Jewett's
bouquet.

II *The Sketch-Stories*

Between the sketch and the short story there exists in Miss
Jewett's writings a hybrid form which exhibits elements of both
yet is legitimately neither. It exudes more action than befits a
true sketch and not enough crucial revelation for a short story.
The desultory walk or ride is not the *raison d'être* of the piece;
the walk or ride serves as impetus to a primary incident or
anecdote. "An Autumn Holiday" (1880) is an early exemplifi-
cation of this genre.

This seasonal idyll has the caprice of starting with a walk and
ending with a drive. In the interim, Miss Jewett's divulgence of
nature's infinitesimal facets imparts again the magic of renew-
ing or extending the reader's own acquaintance with environment. After extracting full measure of ecstasy from her prob-
ings "between the roads," she turns in at the house of Miss Polly
Marsh for respite and conversation. She then presents the most
common of Jewett types—the elderly spinster and the widow—
in Miss Marsh and in her visiting sister, Mrs. Snow. They look
and dress and move alike; indeed, they go together "like a pair
of horses." As they sit spinning, they talk without pause. What

emerges, as Miss Jewett listens appreciatively, is a cataract of gossip followed by a detailed account of the aberration of Dan'el Gunn, which of course recalls several other episodes. The arrival of Dr. Jewett puts an abrupt stop to the flow. This procedure rests on the endless, deflective tradition of Down East yarning, but it certainly owes something to its lustier counterpart of the western frontier. As a matter of fact, "An Autumn Holiday" is a not too distant cousin of the comic form brought to flower in Twain's "The Celebrated Jumping Frog of Calaveras County."

More important than form, however, is the condition of Dan'el Gunn and what it implies about Maine history and humanitarianism. Dan'el is one of Miss Jewett's more indulgent portraits of native oddity, but a mordant report, nevertheless, on the direction and degree of rural degeneration. The contemporary rumor that in the upper storey of every New England farm lived the queer member of the family springs strongly to mind. Dan'el Gunn, a captain of militia in his day, never recovers full mental capacity after a sunstroke. Soon he succumbs to the conviction that he is in fact his sister Patience, now dead five or six years. He begins to wear her clothes and to emulate her activities, first at home, later at church and at a meeting of the Female Missionary Society. This delusion becomes so deep-set that, when the widower deacon visits Dan'el's nephew on a matter of business, Dan'el insinuates the deacon has used this as a subterfuge to come a-wooing him.

Miss Jewett, who accentuates the farcical, seems generally impervious to the darker inferences in this situation. Gunn's breakdown represents the breakdown of masculinity in the region. In assuming the dress and prerogatives of a woman, he stages a retreat from reality, from the obligations a once virile society demanded of a man. His transformation is a step beyond that usually undergone by his generation, for failure to overcome economic or environmental forces is largely reflected by Miss Jewett through debility of spirit or the inutile routines of beached captains. Gunn's female attire, badge of the weaker sex, signifies contempt (perhaps unconscious) on the part of Miss Jewett as she gauges the immense difference between her contemporary male acquaintances and the men who initiated the great tradition she adores. And her contempt is perhaps not so unconscious. Too many men in her sketches and stories, nearer to the norm than Dan'el, do not merely yearn but actually consummate their desire to usurp the position and duties of the opposite sex. Too many women with "faculty" take over a man's work and succeed where he faltered. To mention only one of each: Wilson in "Tom's Husband" and Polly in "Farmer Finch." Both titles commemorate the transfiguration.

Miss Jewett's overt attitude toward male deterioration is the same as the community's. When Dan'el's perverted inclination first appears, the doctor tells people to humor him. When it becomes obvious that it is not a passing fancy, they pity him but cannot help laughing. But they show him every respect and go along with his abnormality, for a commendable protective instinct is at work: the impulse of the clan to shield its feebler segments from harm or ridicule. The remarkable characteristic about Dan'el's collapse, however, is that it excites only comedy and pathos within the group, and not for very long. "The neighbors got used to his ways, and land! I never thought nothing of it after the first week or two," says Miss Marsh. It was apparently no novelty in the long deterioration of the race. They have lived with the rhythm of the tides and so accept the fact of "Miss Dan'el Gunn." Man rises and man falls. They take what life offers and do what they can. Gunn's condition has all the signs of an impotence neurosis deepened into schizophrenia, with complications of transvestism and necrophilia. It is shrugged off by the villagers as a negligible idiosyncrasy; they had neither mind nor stomach for psychiatric quiddities.

Extraneous framework and lack of dramatic spark remove "An Autumn Holiday" from consideration with "The Dulham Ladies," a superior short story of similar drift. This is also true of "The Courting of Sister Wisby," (1887) which must be classified as a hybrid sketch-anecdote. Again Miss Jewett embarks on a holiday *al fresco*, noting weather, flora and fauna with pictorial adroitness as she hops fences and heads over pasture and hill. In the course of her wandering she spies an old friend, Mrs. Goodsoe. Thereafter, a lopsided conversation ensues, with Mrs. Goodsoe doing most of the talking and Miss Jewett acting the prompter at such points where the former seems about to lag. When the essential tale has been told, Miss Jewett resumes her stroll, impressing a familiar cyclical design on her afternoon's outing.

Mrs. Goodsoe's name lends itself to allegorical interpretation—good soul—an epithet Miss Jewett narrowly averts several times. Mrs. Goodsoe epitomizes the physical and spiritual virtues dearest to Miss Jewett's concept of the self-reliant, self-respecting New England matron. She is rather thin, with twinkling eyes in a wrinkled brown face, clear-minded, outspoken, frugal, and famous for her knowledge of herbs. So profound is her affiliation with nature that she has come to look "as if she had properly dried herself, by mistake, with some of her mullein leaves," and frequently she merges into the landscape. Her talk is tangy and studded with parochial wisdom. In many of these aspects and in her great veneration for her mother, Mrs. Goodsoe is distinctly a forerunner of Almira Todd, the resident-spirit of Dunnet Landing.

As the two friends move about snipping mullein, Mrs. Goodsoe looses a barrage of critical commentary on things modern. First she attacks young doctors as "book-fools" who depend upon patent medicines instead of nature's firsthand remedies. Then she denounces railroads and telegraphs, which she considers disruptive of the old, closed social order. The essay at this point takes on the lines of a debate, for Mrs. Goodsoe champions the usages of the past while Miss Jewett inserts enough defense of the present day to keep discussion going. Knowing Miss Jewett's antiquarian propensity, the reader accepts her expedient role as devil's advocate. With drollery and gentle mockery, she disparages the position she has taken: "We were kneeling side by side now, as if in penitence for the march of progress." However, she leaves no doubt that the price of technological progress is spiritual decay.

Mrs. Goodsoe's rebuttals gradually veer into retrospective glimpses at some of her colorful contemporaries, and the longest of these has to do with the hilarious preliminaries to the nuptials of Sister Wisby and Deacon Brimblecom. Sister Wisby is one of Miss Jewett's strong-minded women who do not permit convention to interfere with their plans. The comic ambiguity of the title—"The Courting of Sister Wisby"—is quickly dispelled by Mrs. Goodsoe's explanation: "The way he come a-courtin' o' Sister Wisby was this: she went a-courtin' o' him." Sister Wisby is an authoritative character in her own right, but Mrs. Goodsoe develops into a subjective reaffirmation of regional ideals. Miss

Jewett re-creates the genius of the place through her patience, petulance, joviality, shrewdness, and compassion. Despite this consignment of general attributes, Mrs. Goodsoe retains the uniqueness of a vivid individual. One may apply as wisely to Miss Jewett the verdict of Mencken on Ring Lardner: "He knew that a good character sketch is always a good story, no matter what its structure."

"The Landscape Chamber" (1887), last of the hybrid sketches to be discussed, is Miss Jewett's most distinguished formal accomplishment in the genre. She mounts her horse and rides eastward with no definite goal but to enjoy an extended excursion. What differentiates this adventure from others of its kind is that she completely integrates herself with the drama of the central occurrence, not merely as an acute spectator or auditor but as an actor in fact. She rides out of reality into an island of unreason, immerses herself in its atmosphere, then rides back to the prosaic realm of everyday. She conserves a sense of detachment before and after the strange interlude, but while it lasts she undergoes total involvement.

On the third or fourth day out, the horse suffers a strained foot. Hereafter, the tone and circumstances befit Poe, Hawthorne, and Anne Radcliffe more than they do Sarah Orne Jewett. Specifically, one is reminded of "The Fall of the House of Usher," "The Tell-Tale Heart," *The House of the Seven Gables*, "The Bosom Serpent," and *The Mysteries of Udolpho*. The lone rider approaches a fearful, soundless mansion in which a man and woman live bound together by some uncanny secret. In time, the narrator yields to an indefinable suspicion of footfalls, receives an eerie visitation while lying on a long-unused, curtained bedstead, and is gripped by a sudden terror of isolation. There is an ancestral curse and "a gnawing reptile of shame and guilt and evil memory." The air quivers with sensations uncommon to Miss Jewett: "a thrill of vague apprehension," "a creeping horror."

Through this dilapidated estate and its hapless occupants, Miss Jewett presents one of her most vehement contrasts between past and present. The somber house, which covers the "awful stagnation and hindrance of the processes of spiritual life and growth," is as powerful a character as that in Poe's tragic account of Roderick and Madeline Usher. The landscape chamber keeps scabrously alive a vision of the splendor that once reigned. The oval panel above the empty fireplace depicts a brilliant group of ladies and gentlemen enjoying the luxurious hospitality of the household—a terrible parody of its current position.

The master of the house is a threadbare old man who has evidently known refinement and who still wears the stamp of dignity. When Miss Jewett berates him for his miserliness, he justifies himself on the score of Calvinistic determinism—he wishes to be generous but is restrained by "some power." With frightening passion, he swears at the doom brought upon him by an ancestor whose greed for gain has passed from generation to generation: "We are all in prison while we are left in this world,—that is the truth; in prison for another man's sin." Convinced of his irrationality, Miss Jewett, knowing it to be wasted, nonetheless puts in a word for God's love and free will.

The old man's daughter has grown to dry middle age in bondage to this obsession. Longing for a confidante but dedicated to her father, she is caught between friendliness and defensive seclusion. She entreats and retreats. Her acquiescence to his monomania is so conclusive that Miss Jewett wonders whether she is "the victim or the upholder of her father's traits." When Miss Jewett tries to disengage her from the snare of the old man's delusions, the daughter pleads a promise she made to her mother that she would have patience with him. The deeper truth lies in the fact that, whether through identical weakness or lifelong indoctrination, she too believes they share a miserable doom.

Thus both father and daughter show the taint of time on an erstwhile proud and notable family. The overwhelming pathos of this pair lies in their essential goodness. The old man exhibits an inherent love of horses, is eagerly agreeable at mealtimes, and otherwise resists the tyranny of his inclinations. The daughter's sweet womanliness often breaches her high wall of obduracy. Aware of this dichotomy, Miss Jewett reasons with each of them but is met with his excited outbursts or her quiet resignation. Against the father's argument of inexorable hereditary destiny she opposes the doctrine of redemptive Christianity. She leaves, however, persuaded that neither will make any practical protest against the continuous ebb of vitality from their lives. As the daughter foresees it, "father and the house and I, all three" will one night sink into their own particular tarn. Their disaster is as predictable as that of the Ushers, since this "ancestral dwelling" is imminently "ready to tumble about their ears."

Sarah Jewett produced some of her best mobile character sketches after "The Landscape Chamber." These she encased in the narrative scheme of *The Country of the Pointed Firs* and in the sequel, "The Queen's Twin," which are treated in the category of the novel. Until her final writing days, moreover, Miss Jewett found the attractions of the sketch too great to withstand. In chapters XVI-XVII of *The Tory Lover* (1901), Mary Hamilton mounts a horse and drives through the fields of Berwick with precisely the same enthusiasm and acuity Sarah Jewett displays in earlier cross-country expeditions. Mary reviews the topography and history of the region, talks with a mother and child, evokes the pleasures of childhood, comes to a depressed farmhouse, and lets that rare "remnant of another time," Master Sullivan, characterize himself through a long, intermittent monologue.

Though repetitive procedures seem to flourish in Miss Jewett's numerous sketches, no hint of formula assails the reader. A stimulating freshness and flexibility inform each new *essai* into nature or humanity, for the sketch is a vesture into which she slips with utter comfort. The looseness of its outlines offered ample room for her distinctive temperamental talents and made no rigid demands upon her undeveloped sense of dramatic action. The fiction for which she is remembered owes more to the intimate tone, the peerless characterization, and the philosophic attitudes evolved in the sketches than to any conventional requisites of the narrative art.

Miss Jewett's independent sketches, delectable in themselves, constitute an illuminating introduction to her finest attributes as a writer. They should be read before the more celebrated short stories and novels.

CHAPTER 5

Technique and Temperament

E XCLUSIVE OF THOSE intended for children, Sarah Orne
Jewett published over one hundred short stories in periodicals and newspapers; she collected some seventy of them in nine
volumes (see *Selected Bibliography*). A number of the stories
appear for the first time in these books since editors did not
always agree with Miss Jewett's opinion about her best work.
Tales of New England (1890) is a compilation of eight stories
from four pre-existent collections.

Miss Jewett's career as a writer of short stories began in
January, 1868, when she was eighteen years old, with the publication of "Jenny Garrow's Lovers." Her stock rose precipitously
less than two years later with the appearance of "Mr. Bruce" in
the *Atlantic Monthly* (December, 1869). Excepting "Miss Sydney's Flowers" of July, 1874, she concentrated on sketches and
juvenilia until 1878, the year she inaugurated a broader flow of
stories for adults. The fifteen years from 1885 through 1899
mark her most continuous and significant success, for during
this period she wrote all the short stories now considered her
highest achievement. Her disabling accident in 1902 enforced
a curtailment of output, but it is symptomatic that she published her least effective book and wrote no short work of first
importance in the twentieth century.

From the start, Miss Jewett experienced little or no trouble
shaping the familiar essay into a vehicle suitable to her special
needs. The short story, however, posed more intricate, less amenable problems, and a choice between technique and temperament. On one hand she faced urgent editorial clamor for plot;
on the other, her own desires and shortcomings. She never quite
fulfilled academic requirements for the short story—certainly not
Poe's or Henry James's—nor did she often perform with unsullied

excellence. But in time she came to terms with the genre and produced at least ten stories admissible to any selection of America's best.[1]

Her first stories, formal exercises imitative of current magazine standards, are overplotted, savorless, and disposed to gratuitous homily. Characters and conversation are unbelievably stilted. Locale is generalized, exerting no appreciable effect upon people or situation. Coincidence is the prime mover of action. Gradually, the moods and themes, the environment and inhabitants of the sketches take possession. Plots become less complicated, dialogue more supple, and characters the credible residents of the region. Home-grown interlocutors, speaking the sinewy vernacular, interpret nuances that might escape the uninitiated outlander.

With the collection *A White Heron* (1886), Miss Jewett reaches a perigee of quality, which she regains in *Strangers and Wayfarers* (1890). Her prose is leaner in these volumes, her native parlance more incisive. She places greater dependence upon dialogue and less on narrative maneuver. Girlish interjections fall away. Her insights are keener and her themes subtler. Although she clings to the fault of didactic declaration, she presses fewer theses. Character, simply but indelibly portrayed, is the mainstay. Her grasp of craftsmanship is unmistakably surer in these and subsequent stories. She has made her compromises with necessity and has settled for a form congenial to her abilities yet not exactly a short story. She is now less and less like anyone else and almost purely Jewett.

Miss Jewett's talent for the prescriptive short story was limited, as she well knew. In a letter which mirrors Walter Scott's tribute to Jane Austen's minute art, Miss Jewett disclaims any aptitude for the "good big Harper's story," and allows that she likes to "nibble all round her stories like a mouse."[2] She is disposed to dwell upon the trivialities and commonplaces of simple country people—a round of existence which defies dynamic treatment but which she nevertheless considers equal in importance to the regards of state or the qualms of kings.

Her defect of narrative skill and vigor is the commonest critical complaint. In her earlier stories, before she divests herself of overwrought plots, the critical reader is made uncomfortable by the unwieldiness of her manipulations. Charles Miner Thompson calls some of these "trig social comedies," but even in these

Miss Jewett demonstrates no dexterity in raising action or emotion to satisfactory pitch. Warner Berthoff suggests that the blame may be laid at the feet of Flaubert.[3] However, if a culprit is to be assigned, one must look into Miss Jewett's own temperament. She had a Jamesian aversion to violence—suicide, murder, rape, raving dementia, or other spectacular disorders do not agitate her stories. Reports of turbulent misdoings occur infrequently, and then in the mode of classical tragedy; the actual events are relegated offstage. Her two most horrendous scenes are the fistfight between Dennis Call and Dan Nolan in "Between Mass and Vespers" and the stabbing of Roger Wallingford in *The Tory Lover*.

The later stories, which reflect her victory over mere technique, are practically devoid of plot. A sequence of events is readily evident, but it does not necessarily move toward a revelatory climax. The single incident which betrays in a flash an aspect of character, or a man's knowledge of himself, or a man's relation to his universe is not part of Miss Jewett's repertory. She favors, instead, ordinary instances in the lives of ordinary people: a lonely holiday, a trip to town, a father's doubts, a family leave-taking, a train ride.

Her principal concern is not action but character—more precisely, the interpenetration of character and environment; moreover, the long, slow, internal relevancies develop without galvanic stimuli. And the requirements for her measured analysis of the works and ways of rural New England are quite as modest. She once told Willa Cather that "when an old house and an old woman came together in her brain with a click, she knew that a story was under way."[4] Miss Jewett's conception of a story was not acceptable in all quarters. "A more positive story," pleaded Horace Scudder, who hoped she would cultivate the power of invention, "a more positive story."

Any attempt at definitive classification of Miss Jewett's short stories must end in meaningless duplication. Not many are unilateral in effect, and most simply refuse to submit to the confinement of a single label. Miss Jewett has her limitations, but variety is not one of them. From her full stores of experience and disposition she lifts apposite materials and utilizes them without punctilious regard for continuity of action or mood. What she produces is not a hodge-podge but a loosely coupled train of incidents and impressions.

Miss Jewett's stories cover city locale and characters, are based upon anecdotes and local legendry, and show nature's influence silently at work. Most profuse are her stories about women: the self-possessed spinsters, the lonely or impoverished widows, and their lingering or late romances. She studies young men or women either grappling with problems that have defeated their elders or leaving bare acres for fairer prospects. She watches the reactions of natives who return after many years. She celebrates the occasions of civic and religious holidays. She has several brushes with the world of business, tries her hand with the Irish and French-Canadians who have come to New England, and discreetly visits the stricken South.

No strict divisions are observed in the survey that follows. Stories that recommend themselves through likeness of theme, tone, structure, locale, or characterization, are treated in compatible groups. The ultimate consideration is to secure through a full review some measure of Miss Jewett's success and failure in this aspect of her art.

I Her First Story

Miss Jewett never collected "Jenny Garrow's Lovers" (1868), the first story she published, for the same reasons most mature authors blanch at the resurrection of their earliest works. This one-page melodrama contains enough plot for a full-blown novel: a triangular love affair involving two brothers, a sudden death, a presumptive murder, an unjust imprisonment, an astonishing revival, and the death of all the principals. The action advances spasmodicaly, the language creaks with clichés of the day, and the characters are sticks picked up and dropped at will. Pathos is unrestrained. In short, Miss Jewett produced a typical example of youthful indiscretion.

This story adds nothing to Miss Jewett's stature, but it does display several proclivities which appear in her later writing. First, the scene is laid in her beloved England during the first decade of the nineteenth century. The hunting aristocracy is brought into the fringes of the situation, with every deference to titles and privileges. Second, the story is recounted in a frame of reminiscence by an old woman. This of course stems from Miss Jewett's childhood, listening to tales spun by her grandparents and the retired captains. It appealed to her, then and afterward, that stories do not simply happen; they are told. In the first and last paragraphs, the narrator speaks to the reader entirely out of context. Third, with nice petulance the narrator expresses Miss Jewett's innate distaste for "stories which one sees in all the magazines," written by "those young men and women who use such long words, and have the same story over and over again, with different names." Miss Jewett plainly knew what she wanted from the start even though, at eighteen, she had not yet the talent or the self-assurance to attain it.

II *Stories of the City*

She was volubly prouder of "Mr. Bruce" (1869), her second printed story. One wonders not only why she thought so well of this clumsy, unoriginal parlor farce-romance but why Howells accepted it for the *Atlantic Monthly* in the first place. Kitty Tennant masquerades as a serving-girl in her father's home. Thereupon follows a hoary succession of concealed identity, bewildered lover, marriage, and happy life thereafter. The atmosphere is meant to convey vivacious sophistication, but Kitty's banter shows more girlish strain than Restoration wit. Characterization is shallow and coincidence rife.

Structurally, this is Miss Jewett's most tangled story. It is narrated by Elly, who heard it from Aunt Mary, who relays it through the words of her friend Margaret, who quotes Kitty's letters at length. No gain in depth or range is perceptible. The effect of this excess of apparatus is periodic confusion on the part of the reader as to just who is addressing him. The story comes to a neat close although neither Elly nor Aunt Mary is permitted to bring it full circle. Despite the inordinate shifting of centers, Miss Jewett's fluency of style begins to emerge. Background and language are conventionally rendered; they were not at this time firmly a part of her acquaintance. Miss Jewett's familiarity with big cities deepens considerably in the next ten years but her inability to portray metropolitan life and characters persists. A curious stiffness assails her whenever she attempts to reproduce any but her native places and people.

Even the genteel upper class of Boston in the 1870's could not have been as frangible as she makes it in "A Sorrowful Guest" (1879). When not treating her own environment, she seems helpless to avoid mechanical plots and top-heavy organization. This lurid story of Whiston's misadventures and death would have been more effective without all the technical folderol. Helen Ainslie is the primary narrator. After a lengthy introduction, she learns some odd facts about Whiston, protagonist of the basic story. Before long Helen surrenders her position to him with this lumbering device: "And this is the story he told." Then she resumes her role and brings the sorry tale to a close.

The opening pages indicate possible development into a Jamesian contrast of international social and moral values. Helen, who has lived in Europe since childhood, comes to her brother's house in Boston. But the story veers into subregions of terror and fantasy, for Whiston is one of Poe's pale and fated heroes in the grips of monomania, opium, and hallucinations. Another sharp turn is taken when the supernatural visitations which finally destroy him are rationally explained. Helen concludes with a chaste disquisition on the wages of sin and crime. Such facile pieties, which often hold the thematic kernel, never wholly disappear from Miss Jewett's work. In this she emulates Hawthorne, as she does in her recognition of the intrinsic separateness of human beings. In the case of Helen and her brother, however, she dissolves rather than aggravates the incommunicability.

"A War Debt" (1895), essentially a story of the South, should also be discussed here because the functional character is a Boston gentleman. The first two chapters exude an aura of Old World amenity as Tom Burton dines and chats elegantly with his grandmother. There is much manly reference to cigars and shooting, but Tom is refined to the edge of effeminacy. These qualities, and his immense respect for his grandparent, personate Miss Jewett's ideal of the male aristocrat and his customary concerns. Such a vapid portrait is completely in consonance with her maidenly image of *haut monde* in that nave of Victorian culture.

She acclaims Boston as a center of discriminate living, although cities in general exemplify to her the worst of man's unsocial and immoral impulses. Brash and callous New York is always suspect. Even in the amiable jape, "Fame's Little Day" (1895), the rising metropolis is portrayed as offensively self-satisfied and archly derisive of solid countryfolk. In this story Mr. Pinkham, a small maple-sugar producer from Vermont, comes to New York with his wife on a business–pleasure trip. An impressionable young reporter, intrigued by their rusticity, writes an account of their arrival which inspires other reporters to embellish his version beyond all reason. Next morning, Abel Pinkham, Esquire, emerges as a distinguished entrepreneur in New York on important affairs connected with the maple-sugar industry, a visit of much interest in business and civic circles. Incidental to the dilation of this hoax, Miss Jewett vents a number of objections to the city, some trivial, some grave.

Pinkham winces as he remembers a previous stay during which he had been gulled unmercifully. Mrs. Pinkham's dreams of dignified, distinctive New York City evaporate as she observes some boisterous "young women of forward behavior" and other garish street scenes. Miss Jewett's most serious indictment of the city, however, is concealed on the dark flank of her gentle satire. The Pinkhams, initially homesick and disdainful of New York's attractions, gradually become enamored of themselves and the city as they swallow the cumulative flatteries of the cynical journalists. "I never did have such a splendid time in all my life," declares Mrs. Pinkham, flustered by what she thinks is great respect. These thoroughly duped, bucolic innocents are caught up in a whirligig of delusion which transforms and inverts their values for a fleeting period. In the end, the original reporter wonders what effect this event will have on their future lives.

Miss Jewett chooses to exert the comic element—the irony that, although bamboozled, the Pinkhams enjoy themselves when they would have been relatively miserable. The reverse, of course, suggests itself: what dire wounds the city can inflict when it is not in a laughing mood; how dangerous it is for babes of the woods to wander unchaperoned through the fulsome alleys. The city's scars are almost invariably visible on the integrity of rural visitors or immigrants.

III *Country Yarns*

At the other extreme from Miss Jewett's hyper-plotted and pseudo-sophisticated city stories are the unaffected yarns she heard by wayside or seashore. These are mainly humorous in tone and anecdotal in form. Having the advantage of familiar language, customs, and characters, they come much nearer Miss Jewett's true capacity than those discussed above. A rich lode of localisms run through them, and themes follow the lines broached in the sketches.

"Miss Debby's Neighbors" (1884) recounts several escapades
—hilarious, violent, petty—of the Ashby family in a manner described as "going round Robin Hood's barn." The narrator introduces Miss Debby, then lets her tell the story in all the peculiar-
ity of her own style. The narrator ventures a parenthetical remark or two but avoids returning at the conclusion. This is a
wise retirement, for it permits the melodic accents of Miss Debby's language to linger, rather than jolting the reader immediately out of the fabricated world.

Miss Debby, one of that "class of elderly New England
women which is fast dying out," is a lively relic of the "fast-
disappearing order of things." A tailoress famed for her skill,
she is overtaken by age and by machines that turn out cheap,
ready-made clothes. Her ways are old-fashioned, she has a huge
fund of country lore, and is valued for her "wise reflections and
. . . quaint humor." The last two traits she quickly substantiates.
She forthrightly scolds railroads for "making everybody look and
act of a piece." To this individualist of the old school, conform-
ity and anonymity are affronts to personality, which in her time
was nurtured in virtual isolation and esteemed for its special
fruits. Removal from the land and the gregarious new occupations have helped to destroy the rugged insistence on self which
was the cornerstone of rural character. Progress is measured
in money, not morals. The gist of this plaint is a familiar one
in Miss Jewett's lexicon.

One is tempted to impute the humor of this and other Jewett
stories in this vein to western and southern traditions of interminable, digressive yarning. Certainly "Miss Debby's Neighbors" admits many elements of the Davy Crockett–John Henry frontier
tall tale. Harte, Twain, Cable, Murfree, Eggleston, Page, and less
imaginative local colorists had modified much of the tall tale's
early coarseness and by now (1884) it had become a staple of
magazine fiction. But it must be remembered that a similar, if
less rambunctious, genre had long flourished in the snowbound
farmhouses and country stores of Maine. Miss Debby's accounts
of the six-quart pail and the preserve jar, the house on the
heater-piece, the jug of gin in the well, and the house on the
railroad tracks are in keeping with both the New England and
western–southern oral legacies of dead-pan exaggeration. One
of Miss Jewett's saltiest old codgers, Miss Debby's speech and
attitudes promulgate the essence of rural New England. With

gleam in eye and tongue in cheek, she qualifies as a sprightlier sister to Mrs. Goodsoe, the hardy earth-figure in "The Courting of Sister Wisby."

"The News from Petersham" (1884) is another snippet from the public domain of anecdote—the gossip item blown out of all proportion as it passes from mouth to mouth. Daniel Johnson's touch of common cold is progressively overstated until he is falsely reported dead. The tale comes home to roost when Mrs. Peak, who gave the rumor its first flight, goes to attend the funeral and discovers that Johnson is working briskly among his grapevines. Miss Jewett adds little to this minnow-to-whale story. As compared to others like them in the Jewett gallery, Mrs. Peak and her niece Martha are rather routinely sketched in.

Eight years later Miss Jewett reverts to this comical return-from-death plot, but with infinitely greater success. The air of anecdote is absent from "The Passing of Sister Barsett." The treatment of background and character is fuller and sturdier. Mercy Crane, a fastidiously self-sufficient widow respected by her neighbors, is known to be "a peculiar person" very set in her ways and with pronounced views. She lives in her own neat two-storied house on the Ridge Road, which to her is a stream of provincial news into which she dips when a promising tidbit floats by.

One afternoon she accosts Sarah Ellen Dow, a dependent "watcher" of sick neighbors, and learns that perennially ailing Sister Barsett has finally yielded up the ghost. In her avidity to hear all the particulars—for Miss Dow "sat" till the end—Mrs. Crane invites her into the house, prepares a delectable tea, and induces her to make further revelations. Sarah, gratified by "this handsome social attention" which is a rarity for Mrs. Crane, obliges. When, eventually, it comes out that Sister Barsett has only sustained another "one of her spells," Sarah retreats in a kind of daze; Mrs. Crane collapses with laughter.

The bulk of the story issues from the incisive, idiomatic conversation between Mrs. Crane and Miss Dow. Miss Jewett displays remarkable insight into the minds and matters of women through the quick swipes of vilification they take at the weaknesses of the supposed corpse, never once breaking step or owning to each other what they are doing. The premature post-mortem is inherently funnier because they must now revise their attitudes toward the live and very formidable Sister Barsett. She and her covetous sisters are ugly daguerreotypes of New England's pinched and querulous elderly countrywomen.

The punctilios of back-country Maine become apparent in the artful dodging of Mrs. Crane and Miss Dow who, though equal in feminine foxiness, do not occupy the same social level. Miss Dow's maneuvers for sympathy and invitations are admirably adroit, but Mrs. Crane just as shrewdly eludes them. Miss Dow manages an excellent supper with her misinformation, and Mrs. Crane is as amused by her own credulous liberality as she is about the bogus report. Curiosity may kill cats but it also breaks down social barriers.

One other example of the folk-anecdote should be mentioned if only because it borders on Mark Twain's round-the-belly-stove, yarn-swapping tradition. "The Coon Dog" (1898) retells the adventure of the touted young hound who sneaks off to slumber comfortably at the hearth while the retired old dog actually trees the coon. In Miss Jewett's hands the masculine tone is, of course, modulated. Also, in old Rover's efficacy one may suspect a sly endorsement of past over present generations. More important is her masterly shifting of emphasis from a tale of canine defection to a delineation of basic native character. Mrs. Price is utterly at one with her environment. She exists by her wits and her neighbors' good will: "She ain't had no visible means o' support" for years but gets on snugly by inveterate borrowing. There is nothing of the beggar's slink about her; she is beguilingly forward about educing offers and siphoning gifts. "'Tain't much for a well-off neighborhood like this to support that old chirpin' cricket," says an indulgent farmer. Her ready humor and expansive acknowledgment of her situation have earned her a privileged status in the community.

IV Local Legendry

Miss Jewett deals in local legendry of larger consequence than these antic episodes. Much of it is interstitial, useful to moods or themes: the ominous house in "The Landscape Chamber," the two pines in "A Neighbor's Landmark," and John Paul Jones in *The Tory Lover*. Two short stories, however, may be examined primarily as vehicles of regional lore. "Lady Ferry" and "The Gray Man" are chronicles "that have burned themselves into the cold rocks," the kind that are "slowly magnified and told

to strangers or to wide-eyed children by the dim firelight."[5] Miss
Jewett steeps these stories in tantalizing mystery and a vast love
of the past, rousing frequent echoes of Irving, Poe, and Hawthorne. Although both stories were rejected by the *Atlantic
Monthly*, Miss Jewett thought highly enough of them to include
them in her collected work.[6]

"Lady Ferry" (1879) owes its origin to an old house, an old
cousin, and an old book. In the same way that Hawthorne's
poking into colonial annals initiated so many of his short stories
(or Browning's purchase of the "square old yellow book" in a
Florence bookstall led to *The Ring and the Book*), Miss Jewett's
affection for "a dusty, odd-shaped little book" containing "the
marvellous story of one Mistress Honor Warburton, who was
cursed, and doomed to live in this world forever" gave impetus
to the creation of Lady Ferry. The house is reproduced from
an actual dwelling, and the narrator Marcia is named after a
Jewett cousin.

One of Miss Jewett's most entertaining and sheerly exciting
stories, it is based upon the exploits of a crazed grandam of immense age and indeterminate genesis. To the child Marcia she
mutters familiarly about historic figures now dead over a century.
Other clues indicate that she, a sibling to the Flying Dutchman
and the Wandering Jew, is fated to live endlessly in the world.
Marcia, now adult, tells her story with a mixture of childishness
and maturity which permits her to appreciate the macabre atmosphere while mitigating its fearful effects.

The enigma of Lady Ferry is unfolded skilfully—as a child
might become aware of it—through overheard whispers of parents, brief data from cousins, a chance meeting with the subject,
prattling with a housemaid, and close personal acquaintance.
The mechanically symmetrical structure has a pedagogical introduction of theme, a development of the child's experience,
and a reprise which catches up loose ends. The style is too
mild and the narrative line too limp to hold together the horrific
elements. Gothic appurtenances are everywhere sensate. Lady
Ferry floats through the antique house and cloistered garden
like a restive Ligeia, leaving faint, unmistakable odors in her
wake. The child abides rustling noises, an encounter in moon-
light, a sham funeral, and bats flying. The phrase "endless life"
tolls somberly through the text. The ghostly ball and Lady
Ferry's levitation evoke Washington Irving's folktales. Haw-

thorne's techniques of purposeful ambiguity and multiple choice help to keep the riddle going.

Behind the purely titillating aspects of the story lurks Miss Jewett's unceasing respect for the past. Lady Ferry embodies the accumulated history of ten centuries of culture—"I have lived a thousand years," she says—the culture of queens and captains so dear to Miss Jewett. But she does not allow fancy to erase reality. With the grimness of Swift contemplating his Struldbrugs, Miss Jewett asserts:

> We have an instinctive fear of death; yet we have a horror of a life prolonged far beyond the average limit: it is sorrowful; it is pitiful; it has no attractions.
>
> This world is only a schoolroom for the larger life of the next. Some leave it early, and some late: some linger long after they seem to have learned all its lessons. This world is no heaven: its pleasures do not last even through our little lifetimes.
>
> There are many fables of endless life, which in all ages have caught the attention of men; we are familiar with the stories of the old patriarchs who lived their hundreds of years: but one thinks of them wearily, and without envy.

Nowhere in her writings does Miss Jewett come so close to pessimism. She unreluctantly accedes that old times, no matter how rich and fulfilling, must eventually give way to new. This she dramatizes through one of Lady Ferry's leading eccentricities, the periodic sacrament of her own funeral. Troubled by the ghastly skull that underlies even the most beautiful face, Marcia's faith in God wavers for a time. God's assurance is not enough to placate doubts and fears about the final mysteries of existence. Many years later Marcia returns to find that Lady Ferry is unquestionably dead. "I smiled at my satisfaction and at my foolish childish thoughts, and thanked God that there could be no truth in them, and that death comes surely." Doubt is repudiated and folklore put in the employ of Christian orthodoxy.

The origination of "The Gray Man" (1886) reads like an excerpt from Hawthorne's notebook, and its explicit peroration is like his penchant to underscore patent themes. The gray man is the favorite folk figure, Death, in one of his conciliatory disguises. This disguise makes the fearsome experience of death explicable and even familiar—just as the anthropomorphic inclination gives God a body and renders Him conceivable.

The gray man is readily identifiable, for hints are dropped liberally along the way. His uniform color denotes him immediately (and this implied lack of blood differentiates him from Poe's more intense and florid specter in "The Masque of the Red Death"). He appears a man who had "known trouble and perplexity, and was fulfilling some mission that gave him pain; yet saw some gain and reward beyond." Advertently or not, Miss Jewett punningly refers to him as seated like a skeleton beside a fire and as reading gravely in the dead of night.

The story, which moves indolently from historical flashback to current situation, develops a sensed dread of the unknown around a reputedly haunted farmhouse. The gray man comes to live in it and, despite many proffers of aid to his neighbors, is looked upon with instinctive suspicion—*he is never seen to smile.* Like the Reverend Hooper in Hawthorne's "The Minister's Black Veil," he attends a gay wedding party and affects its spirit adversely. Symbolically, he is thrust out of this beginning of a new life, for he represents the end of all life. The bridegroom who shows him to the door is mankind wishing to make Death a permanent outcast, or at least to remove his shadow from present happiness, however transitory. The message is clear: although Death "tries to teach and serve mankind so that he may at the last win welcome as a faithful friend," he is in no form welcome. He cannot endear himself; his fell purpose is eternally obnoxious.

Aldrich may have spurned this story because of its ubiquitous reappearance in oral and printed versions. And then, neat engineer that he was about his own fiction, he may have squirmed at Miss Jewett's abandonment of continuity in her last page. The gray man disappears summarily and is later glimpsed by a wounded farmer's boy in battle—Death himself on a tall horse.

V *The Influence of Nature*

The power of nature to influence human lives physically, morally, and spiritually is a theme twining through four of Miss Jewett's novels, almost all of her sketches, and a majority of her short stories. It crops up to various degrees, but is never very far from the surface. In several of the short stories it ranks as the major consideration in transforming or strengthening individual character. In the following two, nature provides the basis for more fruitful relations with one's fellows.

"Miss Sydney's Flowers" (1874) illustrates the aphorism that one touch of nature makes the whole world kin. Miss Sydney, a wealthy spinster living alone in a stately, dismal house, has gradually shrunk from society as her friends have died and prefers the people she meets in books. While not repressive, she encourages no intimacies, and has the reputation of "a good woman in a negative kind of way." When a newly constructed street along the side of her house exposes her beloved conservatory and garden to the passing public, she is understandably distressed. Step by step, however, she adheres to the people who stop to admire her flowers. First she befriends a pair of pitiful tots and then the old candy-woman and her lame sister; eventually she visits the Children's Hospital rather than merely sending flowers. When she strikes it off with fresh, young Bessie Thorne, her circle of renewal is complete. Through the pleasure her flowers have given others, she is freed from her cell of memories and prejudices. She vows thereafter "to be better,—not alone for the sake of having friends, not alone to quiet her conscience, but because she knew she had been so far from living a Christian life, and she was bitterly ashamed." She has made effective peace with God, with herself, and with humanity—which literally beats a path to her doorstep.

Miss Jewett not only preaches unconscionably throughout this story but also brings some apt analogies into play. Miss Sydney's spiritual regeneration is likened to seeds of kindness and charity sprouting in the empty garden of her heart or to a tree covered with good fruit which is never unnoticed in the fields. And a Wordsworthian moral prodigy overtakes the young man who is turned away from crime by the sight of Miss Sydney's flowers.

The impact of nature is more social than spiritual in "A Neighbor's Landmark" (1894). Against the wishes of his family and the community, John Packer approves the removal of two great pine trees on his property which have served for years as beacons for travelers by land or sea. A perverse man and a trenchant individualist, he does not intervene until the sawyers are on their way. Thereupon, his wife and daughter—who had remained silent though distraught—and his grateful neighbors give him a surprise party. Happy to have saved the trees, gruff John Packer, "who usually hated company," shakes hands with everyone who comes.

The two pines are overt symbols of Packer and his wife. "They always make me think of a married couple," says a fisherman. "I bet you if anything happened to one on 'em t'other would go an' die." By his obstinacy Packer puts a strain on his marital relations, which he realizes at the last moment. The trees "seemed to have taken a step nearer each other, as if each held the other fast with its branches in a desperate alliance." He must preserve the trees if he is to preserve the strength and happiness of his union.

Miss Jewett extends this application through her reliance on a text from Deuteronomy: "Cursed be he that removeth his neighbor's landmark. And all the people shall say, Amen." Packer's secret longing for social approval, hidden beneath a cross and autocratic manner, is unmasked by the threat to the communal pines. His dilemma of self versus society is at the core of the story. Other characters are sketched in strongly—particularly Ferris the contractor, one of Miss Jewett's most despicable countrymen—but none with such finish as Packer.

"What shall I do with my 'White Heron' now she is written? She isn't a very good magazine story, but I love her, and I mean to keep her for the beginning of my next book."[7] It is an irony that Miss Jewett wrote Annie Fields in this vein about what has since become her best known and most anthologized short story. Such diverse personalities as Dr. S. Weir Mitchell and Ellen Terry acclaim it in letters. Mary E. Wilkins Freeman, who compares it with Tolstoi's "Two Deaths," generously declares that she had never written so good a story. Critics in the main bear out Miss Jewett's own high evaluation; for example, Arthur Hobson Quinn reaches zenith in his praise—"Perfect of its kind." Against such panegyric Pattee enters the demurral that "A White Heron" is *too* literary, "too much from the intellect and not enough from the heart." While he swings to an opposite excess, his judgment is instructive.

"A White Heron" (1886) is neither so artlessly simple nor so stylistically pure as it has been made out. Most questionable is Miss Jewett's manipulation of point of view. She has been praised for her objective method and for exposing only enough of Sylvia's mind to gauge the quality of the decision the child ultimately comes to. But Miss Jewett plays several tricks with perspective and violates the detachment of her stance too frequently. She begins as omniscient narrator, recounting her story in the past; shifts suddenly to the dramatic present tense when Sylvia hears the hunter's whistle; reverts to the past almost immediately; addresses Sylvia directly; returns to the present, then again to the past; and closes with a superfluous explanation to the reader. There is too much jostling in the presentation to be worthy of the label "perfect."

As to the meaning, it is not pointed out that for Sylvia the choice between heron and hunter is not affirmation but re-affirmation; it is not resistance to new temptation but final repudiation of accreted evil. Nurtured on material values, this child spends her first eight years in a crowded manufacturing town. Brought to live on her grandmother's farm, she quickly establishes affinity with the green world and its denizens. "There ain't a foot o' ground she don't know her way over, and the wild creaturs counts her one o' themselves," observes her grand-mother. When the young ornithologist offers her ten dollars to reveal the location of the white heron's nest, she is momentarily enticed by the money and suffused by a dream of love for him. These, suggests Miss Jewett, are values of the past life: "Has she been nine years growing and now, when the great world for the first time puts a hand to her, must she thrust it aside for a bird's sake?" Sylvia's conflict, then, is the age-old one between city and country, between flesh and spirit. When she opts for nature, she ratifies a love infinitely deeper than those personified in the sophisticated outsider.

Sylvia also undergoes a rite of initiation, an arduous journey to self-discovery and maturity. The pine tree which towers above all others in the forest attracts her because from its top "could not one see all the world?" Vision beyond the ordinary is her aspiration. She would gaze down upon all the mysteries of nature—and grow in heart as tall as the pine. She starts her climb significantly at dawn. First up the small oak that grows alongside (the apprenticeship youth must serve before ventur-ing higher), then across to the lower branches of the pine, she accomplishes a passage only some will dare. Torn by sharp twigs (the pains of experience), she creeps slowly upward, until she stands triumphant at treetop. It is morning now and clearly in the distance she espies the heron (the elusive meaning of exist-ence). A triple reward is hers: she has achieved knowledge of nature, knowledge of self, and a merger of self with nature. There can be no doubt now. To divulge the secret of the heron would be to divulge the secret of self; to destroy one would be to destroy the other. She does not lead the young man to the nest. She never tells.

VI *Self-Reliant Women*

The primary subject of Miss Jewett's stories is women: young, middling, and old; dependent and self-sufficient; grim and comical; impecunious and well-to-do. They usually face untenable situations and accept them meekly, fight them vehemently, or simply laugh them off. The two most numerous groups are the self-reliant matrons and the impoverished or lonely spinsters and widows. Many of the former are cantankerous domestics who keep impeccable house, are privy to all local arcana, psychologize astutely, play genial despots to and fiercely protect the coddled household. The finest of these self-reliant women are from the middle class, the archetype of whom is Almira Todd. A special pathos attaches to the aristocratic ladies who clench adversity but make no sign to the world.

Horatia Dane of "A Lost Lover" (1878) is one of these. An elderly spinster living on the memory of a remote romance with a sailor who never returned from sea, she is suddenly confronted with him, a lying, begging, disreputable drunkard who does not even recognize her. The fond pretense that has sustained her life is shattered: he had indeed deserted her, not drowned. She rationalizes that "after all, loneliness was not so hard to bear as other sorrows," and she shudders at the thought of the misery she would have endured with him. She lets him go without identifying herself. Little immediate change is noticeable, but she ages rapidly, and her neighbors notice that "she was not the woman she had been a year ago." In her heart of hearts the animating illusion is dead.

Miss Jewett balances accounts in "A Lost Lover" with Horatia's solicitous cook, Melissa. She is the norm of New England provincials, tough, quaint, and sentimental. Her strength, robust rather than neurotic, comes from confidence in aptitude rather than self-delusive reverie. Melissa's language is as gritty as the soil she springs from, with no concessions to local-color picturesqueness.

In another short story Miss Eliza Peck, in a social niche somewhere between these two, suffers desertion similar to Horatia's. Called upon to run temporarily a bereaved minister's parsonage, she performs her duties so satisfactorily that everyone assumes the arrangement will be prolonged through marriage. For a while Eliza herself is bemused by this possibility. When the Reverend Elbury marries another woman, Eliza indignantly refuses to stay on as housekeeper and returns home.

The dramatic development of "Miss Peck's Promotion" (1887) is unusual for Miss Jewett. Eliza talks to herself habitually, not in the way of most solitaries, but as a bifurcated psyche of strong and weak persons—Dr. Jekyll and Mr. Hyde without the great moral gap. "The quailing side of her nature" wants to believe that the minister will marry her, but the staunch side restrains her from making unguarded remarks or taking appearances for granted. Through this technique Miss Jewett successfully charts Eliza's feminine perplexity, her tremulous hopes, her disappointment, outrage, and calm readjustment to the facts of her position. Her "promotion" consists primarily in triumph over the celibate's tendency to be foolish about love in middle age. She has also improved herself culturally during numerous evenings with the minister and can now enjoy her new riches in her natural environment. From her own home on the hillside she can "have a good honest look at yellow sunset." She has gained the best of both worlds.

In both these stories Miss Jewett registers her low opinion of men who have not the sense to grasp the best offered by the community (Reverend Elbury's new wife is "a townish, empty-faced, tiresomely pretty girl" dressed in "conspicuous bad taste"). In each case the rejected woman demonstrates courage and forbearance in the sturdiest tradition of the region. These women are the true saviors of value; the male line has run to seed.

"Law Lane" (1887) is a comic domestication of the Montague–Capulet feud and the Romeo–Juliet entanglement. If the narrative movement is lax, the story is distinguished by several choice characterizations. The young lovers are negligible, but rascally Joel Smith is a Down East Huckleberry Finn. Virulent Mrs. Barnet resembles Sister Barsett in more than name. Lydia Bangs and Mrs. Powder, old friends and rivals (like E. A. Robinson's Isaac and Archibald), savor each other's company as they contend over blueberries. Mrs. Powder is the capstone of the plot. Garrulous, optimistic, generous, and resourceful, she accidentally intensifies the quarrel between families and causes separation of the lovers. Through the exercise of native ingenuity and a brawny sense of humor she manages at one blow to end the feud and reunite the lovers.

The heroines of "A Village Shop" (1888) and "Miss Tempy's Watchers" (1888) are indomitable women in converse ways: the live one is virtually dead and the dead one is virtually alive. Although hardly necessary, Miss Jewett in the first story explicitly associates Esther Jaffrey with Hawthorne's Hepzibah Pyncheon. Esther, descendant of a famous but faded line, opens a small shop in her house in order to support herself and her ineffectual scholar-brother. She undergoes the humiliations of trade and the obloquy of a useless male without plaint, as befits her exalted genealogy. She often regrets not having been born a boy but dares not venture into "unfeminine directions." She is a prisoner of heredity and convention, like the daughter in "The Landscape Chamber," but more out of pride than love. Unable to rescue herself, she flits about her shop like a wraith in a tomb and is a joyless contrast to her brimming schoolgirl clients.

Escape is offered through prosperous farmer John Grant, whose daughter marries the scholar-brother. Esther cannot reconcile herself to indirect dependence upon even this decent yeoman. "*Never!*" she cries to her brother's proposition that she shut up shop. As the story closes, she goes off "stately as a princess" to wait on an early customer. She is one of Miss Jewett's indestructible aristocrats who uphold centuries of gentility upon their frail shoulders in an era indifferent to such traditions. Remembering the magnificent Marlborough Jaffrey, she cannot stoop to the indignity of aid from a social inferior. Bewitched by the past, she cannot come to terms with the present. So she accepts her deprivation with mixed bitterness and gratification: bitter over the anomaly of her irresponsible brother; gratified that she has historic support for insistence upon self.

In "Miss Tempy's Watchers," Miss Tempy Dent lies dead in the north chamber of her home, while Mrs. Crowe and Miss Binson sit in the kitchen on the night before the funeral. Both old schoolmates and friends of Tempy, she had asked them to look after her affairs when she died. As the two women talk, they get the impression of a third person listening: "The watchers could not rid their minds of the feeling that they were being watched themselves." And this is precisely what Tempy had intended.

Of late years the two watchers had fallen away from each other. Wealthy Mrs. Crowe, whose social status was much superior to Miss Binson's, knows exactly what she is about. Although she looks benignant and acts the part, she is actually a niggard. Miss Binson, on the other hand, works her farm and supports six nieces and nephews without whining. Tempy's hope had been to bring them together again, to create a chemistry of better understanding through a period of intimate partnership. As they recall Tempy's multiple virtues, Tempy's spirit becomes a felt arbiter, dissolving differences of rich–poor, stingy–kind, and church faction which lay between them. Before the night is over, Tempy's influence brings humility to Mrs. Crowe, sympathy to Miss Binson, and deeper self-perception to both. "The pale shape of Tempy Dent, the outworn body of that generous, loving-hearted simple soul" accomplishes in death what it had not achieved in life. Essence once more triumphs over existence.

Edward Garnett cites "Miss Tempy's Watchers" as "an epitome of Miss Jewett's talent . . . showing the finest shades of her quality."[8] It is indeed one of her superlative achievements, developed with the homely precision of a Breughel. One by one and gradually the lights in the hearts of three women become distinguishable; one by one the features of an entire community emerge from the surrounding gloom. Miss Jewett's command of atmosphere is matchless; she provides with unobtrusive strokes exactly the kind of background in which death might congenially exchange confidences with life. There is no action, no crisis, merely a conversation which seems to drift aimlessly from one topic to another. "Yet," as Matthiessen says, "it possesses an inevitability."[9]

Mercy Bascom and Betsey Lane, two elderly women in dependent circumstances, assert their independence by taking journeys away from their restricting environs. Mrs. Bascom of "Fair Day" (1888) is one of Miss Jewett's plucky widows who subdues a stubborn, stony farm and brings up four children successfully. Now living at her son's home, she resentfully casts about for something to do when the family drives off to the fair. She decides to visit her own old homestead, which she had reluctantly sold. Finding the owners out, she lets herself in and spends an ecstatic interlude reliving her past life among the familiar walls and furniture. In this mood she begins to reprove herself for the forty-year quarrel she has maintained with her sister-in-law. Where Hawthorne would have turned this situation into a bout of guilt and self-recrimination, Miss Jewett makes it an occasion for spiritual regeneration. Mercy determines to patch it up with her sister-in-law. It has been a "fair" day in more than one context.

Mercy talks constantly to herself, but not as the duple-souled Eliza Peck. Miss Jewett bends this habit to the purpose of exposition and, of course, characterization. Mercy informs us that she enjoys "try'n to cope with things and gettin' the better of my disadvantages." She exclaims pettishly, "I'm as able as most, though I be seventy-three year old." The only chink in her armored self-reliance appears when she tries to convert her son into a surrogate husband after her three daughters have married; she turns "cold with misery and disappointment" when he announces he has found a girl to suit him.

The apparent last fling of Betsey Lane, an aged poorhouse inmate, comprises the superstructure of "The Flight of Betsey Lane" (1893). The interior harbors a tender fable of love and rejuvenation. With a surreptitious gift of money, Betsey slips out of the institution one morning and entrains for the Philadelphia Centennial which she has long yearned to visit. After some futile inquiries, the search for her is terminated. Her two cronies, Peggy Bond and Lavina Dow are at first aggrieved because she did not confide in them; then they begin to worry that she may have taken her life in the nearby pond. Several mornings later they are on their way to investigate, when Betsey emerges briskly from a thicket of alders. The three repair happily to the poorhouse.

Betsey's escapade, like Mercy's, eventuates in the fulfillment of a dream. Philadelphia is not so much the site of a centennial celebration as it is the city of liberty and brotherly love. For Betsey it represents one final declaration of independence, and, through ingenuous delight in the gaudy exhibits, she draws ordinarily apathetic strangers together in companionable interest. Pathos emanates from the contrast of her sprightliness and old age, but it is a subtler sort than that in the closing tableau. Peggy Bond has the unusual malady of "upsightedness" which causes her to trip into brooks and ditches, and Lavina Dow is crippled with rheumatism. One summons up a lithograph of The Spirit of '76 as Peggy lugs Betsey's bundle and basket, while Betsey triumphantly assists Lavina across the wide green field to the

poorhouse. Miss Jewett means this to climax the poignantly genuine love these women bear for each other. Over and above the
sentimentality, they stand as living exemplars of the Christian
principles *love thy neighbor* and *love begets love*. It is one of
Miss Jewett's most delicate successes.[10]

"The Guests of Mrs. Timms" (1894) pits two formidably self-
possessed matrons against each other, but it is more informative
as social comedy than as a *tour de force* of personalities. The
complex ritual of visiting is meticulously and aciduously examined from several levels of protocol, intricacy, and snobbery.
Kipling valued this story more than any of the others in *The
Life of Nancy*, pleased that his three winters in New England
enabled him to extract its full flavor.

Mrs. Persis Flagg is one of Sarah Jewett's most corrosive crea-
tions. She is rude, pretentious, shrewd, hypocritical, arrogant,
presumptuous, deceitful, self-seeking, snobbish, bullying, self-
deluding, avaricious, and contemptible. She prevails on Miss
Pickett, a timidly sincere woman, to take up the invitation
vaguely proffered by Mrs. Timms to visit her home in a neighboring town. When they appear without notice at the front
door, Mrs. Timms lets them cool their heels awhile, then meets
them with a frigid smile. She keeps them at bay in the parlor
by sitting just a little too far away to seem exactly pleasant;
she proposes cake and wine, but makes no move to produce
them. A virtuoso at arm's-length maneuvering, she instantly
seizes on the hint that they must go and ushers them out
cordially, "as if to leave no stone of courtesy unturned." Mrs.
Flagg has met a Tartar.

Outside the house she becomes vituperative. In sheer disappointment she condescends to visit Nancy Fell, who keeps
house for her nephew and thereby rates low in Mrs. Flagg's
social register. Here, ironically, they are immediately set at ease
and served a fine dinner. A scriptural theme rises from the comparison of these two encounters; Nancy Fell "was more generous
with her little than many was with their much."

The story is faultlessly organized around four visits, each with
special implications bearing on the implacable regimen of small-
town New England. The first visit is Miss Pickett's at Mrs.
Flagg's, where it is made dismally plain to Miss Pickett that she
is barely tolerated and that time spent with Mrs. Flagg is a
distinction by no means small. The contrasting second and

third visits to Mrs. Timms and Nancy Fell have been described. The fourth visit, cunningly woven into the total design, mimics the motifs of the Timms and Fell visits. At one of the stage stops during their ride to Mrs. Timms's home, Mrs. Flagg and Miss Pickett notice an unexpected visitor having difficulty gaining entry into the house of a suspicious hostess who neither remembers her very well nor is convinced that she invited her for an extended stay. On the ride back they see the sanguine stranger ensconced beamingly in the window seat, her luggage nowhere in sight—an episode worthy of Dickens. Miss Jewett utilizes this visit as prefiguration of the Timms rebuff, as reprise of the Fell welcome, and as connective thread for the entire fabric.

Miss Jewett's capacity for biting irony is strongly evinced in "The Guests of Mrs. Timms." Mrs. Flagg's discomfiture is prefaced by a series of actions and remarks which, inversely, sink their barbs into her own flesh. Out of deference to Mrs. Timms's social standing, she wears her best black cashmere and carries her fringed parasol. Airily she proclaims to Miss Pickett, "My gracious, won't Mis' Timms be pleased to see us!" and then wonders "what Mis' Timms is likely to give us for dinner." As they wait for Mrs. Timms to open the door, she whispers, "I expect she'll urge us terribly to remain with her over-night"; she has in fact secretly prepared for this contingency by packing her black leather handbag. Before they are repelled by Mrs. Timms, Miss Pickett charitably suggests that they drop in on old Nancy Fell. With visions of grander social conquests in mind, Mrs. Flagg sniffs coldly, "We might just look in a minute; I shouldn't want her to feel hurt." Later she grasps at this possibility in order to palliate her distress over the snub by Mrs. Timms. But she acquires no humility from these experiences. Intransigent as ever, she answers Miss Pickett's grateful tribute to Nancy's "real nice little dinner" with, "She'll enjoy tellin' folks about our comin' over to see her."

"Aunt Cynthy Dallett" (1899) combines the thematic vein of love in "The Flight of Betsey Lane" and the structural ligament of visits in "The Guests of Mrs. Timms." Abby Pendexter loves her friend Mrs. Hand, and they both love Abby's eighty-five-year-old Aunt Cynthy who lives alone on a mountain. Cynthy resists all entreaties that she come down and share her elderly niece's home. Finally she surrenders her lonely self-reliance, but on her own terms—her niece will come up to live with her. Three visits contribute to the mood and movement of the story. In the first, Abby and Mrs. Hand plan their visit to Aunt Cynthy. The second, told in retrospect by Mrs. Hand, is an hilarious but heartwarming visit with one of her friends, which demonstrates the necessity and the rewards of such visits for housebound women. The third visit finds Abby and Mrs. Hand at Aunt Cynthy's, where love of one another shines conspicuously through their conversation. Miss Jewett's attitude is completely sympathetic. Coldness and reluctance dominate most of the visiting in "The Guests of Mrs. Timms"; unseeking concern and touchingly tender love pervade those of "Aunt Cynthy Dallett."

VII *Superannuated Courtships*

In the six years between February 1889 and September 1895 Miss Jewett published seven short stories which center upon the problems and indirections of superannuated courtship. This concerted upsurge was no mere flash in the pan. The vagaries of romantic love among the elderly had long interested her and continued to do so afterward. As early as 1878 she considered the effects of courtship upon brave Horatia Dane ("A Lost Lover"). In 1881 she looked squarely at the preliminaries to marriage that occupy Rebecca Parsons and the Reverend Beacham in "Miss Becky's Pilgrimage." "A New Parishioner," "Marsh Rosemary," "The Courting of Sister Wisby," and "Miss Peck's Promotion" also touch upon love in the yellow leaf, as does "A Dunnet Shepherd-ess." Each of these, however, fixes on other matters or the court-ship is part of a larger scheme. The stories discussed below turn humorously or sentimentally on the wooing activity, except "The Only Rose," which achieves its purpose through recall.

The self-assurance of the women in these affairs comes out in their masterful manipulations. They know what they want and forthwith get it. Miss Jewett has some good female fun over the natural stupidity of the genus male who is usually bagged before he knows he is being stalked. Women, invariably the wilier, conduct a classic strategy while leaving men the illusion that they are planning the battles in the endless war between the sexes.

In "The Quest of Mr. Teaby" (1890), Hannah Pinkham plays a procrastinating game with the old nostrum peddler; she juggles his periodic proposals without a definite yea or nay. She is obviously fond of him and has no intention of giving up the flattery and satisfaction of his attentions. Miss Jewett connotes their degrees of feeling through the diversity of their clothes: Mr. Teaby wears a linen duster "as if it were yet summer," while Hannah is bundled up "as if she expected winter to set in at once." The presence of an eavesdropping narrator is somewhat distracting and inhibits the shy charm of this chance meeting.

"A Winter Courtship" (1889) might well have been titled "The Taking of Jefferson Briley," for he starts his daily seven-mile journey a carefree bachelor and ends it "spoken for." Widow Fanny Tobin boards his passenger-and-mail covered wagon one winter morning and is invited to share the front seat and his buffalo robe. At first awkwardly, then sentimentally, then earnestly, she steers him into a declaration. Briley likes to imagine himself a pony express driver dashing over dangerous Rocky Mountain trails, and Mrs. Tobin cannily exploits this Walter Mitty weakness to her advantage. In this highly effective monochrome Miss Jewett limns imperishably two rockbound New England characters against their accustomed physical and cultural backgrounds.

As a first-rate example of Miss Jewett's comedic art, "Miss Esther's Guest" (1893) has been undeservedly neglected. It brilliantly incorporates the humor and pathos of age, turning a witless contretemps into the beginnings of an inspiriting life for two elderly people. Esther Porley and Mr. Rill are brought together adventitiously, but it soon becomes apparent that they have many attributes in common. They have both lost their mainstays recently (she, a mother; he, a sister); they dress in the old mode; they have the same tastes. An immediate attraction of the lost for the lost sets in. Their winter courtship evolves out of sweetness and *simpatia* rather than thawing frigidity and crafty engineering. The final monosyllabic exclamation is a masterpiece of comic climax, and it comes like four huge bass notes at the end of a lyric played on the harpsichord.

The marvelously efficient heroines of "A Second Spring" (1893) and "The Taking of Captain Ball" (1889) are hired as housekeepers and eventually get their man. The first story is a serious chronicle of the trials of goodhearted Maria Durrant. She is constrained by the still potent influence of her employer's deceased wife and the malignant shafts of the village gossips; but, by sheer desire to make his life happy and restful, she suc-

ceeds in establishing an equal position in his heart. Her great
gratification is to hear him say, "I've got a good wife *now*." The
second story follows similar lines, except that Captain Ball has
never married. Here too the village attitudes are delivered in
Greek chorus fashion by female xenophobes who resent having
so good a catch snatched away. When all conditions seem ripe for
the Captain's surrender, the housekeeper reveals herself as his
niece. Despite the superficial plot, Miss Jewett develops four
characters with infinite care in a latitude of shifting moral and
economic values. Gleefully she lets go a parting jab at the folly
of the male animal. Captain Ball, elated over the surprising
dénouement, still cannot hide from himself the small disappointment that his niece is a widowed matron—he had pictured a
pretty girl in a pink dress. And in this reaction are shades of the
Reverend Elbury who preferred a shallow townish beauty to the
solid worth of Miss Eliza Peck.

In "All My Sad Captains" (1895) Mrs. Lunn has a choice
among three prospective husbands; in "The Only Rose" (1894)
Mrs. Bickford vacillates in a choice among her three dead husbands. Mrs. Lunn, leaving nothing to chance, chooses deliberately
and for romantic reasons. Mrs. Bickford finally thrusts her
dilemma into the hands of fate; fortuitously, the ultimate choice
corresponds with her fondest attachment—romantic love. In
both these stories Miss Jewett provides sufficient characterization of the men to engage the reader in the problem of judgment
or at least give him a rooting interest in one or the other candi-
date. The first story is presented as it occurs; the second unfolds
by retrospect. Both are light in tone; "All My Sad Captains"
leans to farce, and "The Only Rose" is sportively sentimental.
In middle age Miss Jewett votes twice for the trepidations of
young love and against utilitarian courtship and marriage.

Besides telling a merry tale, in each case she ponders a topic
of weightier consequence. The sad captains are surrounded by
palpable signs of decline. Decaying timbers, deserted wharves,
and musty warehouses comprise the shoreline. A passing loco-
motive hoots derisively, cutting through the captains' reveries,
but they do not hear. The possessive pronoun in the title pre-
sages Miss Jewett's nostalgic bias for the past. After much fluctua-
tion, Mrs. Bickford leaves the resolution to her nephew—"John
was smiling fate." Miss Jewett flirts with the idea of an inexplicable power which assumes decision and moves people in

directions apart from their own wills. Since the upshot is almost always for the best, she evidently conceives this force to be beneficent (God) rather than monstrous (Devil). In instances of large moral import she is content to let it prevail.

VIII *Spinsters and Widows*

One other class of elderly women Miss Jewett delineates extensively is the lonely or impoverished spinsters or widows. Living alone or in pairs, they are pathetic whether rich or poor. Time has passed them by and left only some tatters of memories to live on. In an epoch too busy and brash for them to cope with, they fade perceptibly as the light plays over them. One of the few who comes off with banners high is Miss Catherine Spring in "A Late Supper" (1878). Her success, however, depends on a *deus ex machina*. An unlikely coincidence during an inadvertent ride in a railroad car delivers her from dire financial need and makes it possible for her to take in a homeless child. This theme of God moving in mysterious ways his wonders to perform is freighted with Miss Jewett's worst didactic manner. As narrator, she explains the workings of God's providence with Teutonic thoroughness, embellishing her thoughts about "the wonderfully linked-together chain" with quotations from a Sunday sermon and from "Rabbi Ben Ezra."

In "Going to Shrewsbury" (1889) old Mrs. Peet is robbed of her farm by a nephew. Compelled to go to live in the city with one of her nieces, she also takes a train ride. Her fate, however, is left in doubt. The reader learns that she spends a most active and enjoyable winter before she dies, but the testimony is supplied by her scoundrelly nephew. Mrs. Peet is proud of her self-reliance: "I ain't goin' to sag on to nobody," she doggedly asserts. But the symbol of her dissolution is the bundle-handkerchief which comes untied and scatters her belongings over the car floor. The downfall of this honest woman is brought about not by a circumstance in nature or by a fault in herself but by human chicanery. Mrs. Peet's quick death raises another moot inference: How long can country merit survive city environment?

A third solitary, Ann Floyd of "Marsh Rosemary" (1886), meets unqualified defeat. She is a composite of several Jewett–elderly-woman traits. A sensible but susceptible spinster, she decides to marry a considerably younger man—a good-looking, good-natured, spineless loafer about town. She self-reliantly adopts the role of breadwinner, confident she is "the better man of the two." Shortly he abandons her, and she becomes a grass widow. Some time later she discovers him living in a nearby town with a young wife and their child. Rather than destroy the obvious happiness of this household, she reverts desolately to the silence and loneliness of her former status.

Nowhere does Miss Jewett convey the pathos of age with keener poignancy. Ann returns home heartbroken from the scene of radiant young love, knowing hopelessly that the life she sought is beyond her reach, although commonplace to younger folk. She had picked her course with few illusions, out of an ageless hunger, half sure that it would end disastrously. With characteristic fortitude, on the night of her return, she leaves the light off; she wants no well-meaning sympathy from her neighbor in this hideous moment.

When Miss Jewett's elderly spinsters live in pairs, they intensify rather than dilute their miseries. Two old people jointly suffering affliction exert a sum effect greater than one plus one—a calculus of pain familiar to any compassionate eyewitness. This is felt in the hopeless plight of Ann and Mandy Bray in "The Town Poor" (1890). Assigned by public charity to the home of a harassed townswoman, they are visited by two sympathetic friends. The sisters try piteously to entertain in their dreadfully cramped and destitute quarters. Upon leaving, the more sanguine of the visitors declares she will speak to the selectmen about this outrageous situation, as well as encourage some private benefactions.

Neglect of these helpless human beings scrapes the nerves of indignation. Here in its ugliest form is displayed the propensity of individuals and communities to make the least of their obligations, to shove their shame out of sight, to hope perhaps that problems will vanish if not seen or talked about. Miss Jewett seldom takes a stand at the firing line of social reform, but here she lets fly an arrow at "the well-to-do town of Hampden [that] could provide no better for its poor than this." The visitor's optimism is heartening—up to a point. One remembers more vividly the Bray sisters with a single chair between them.

"The Dulham Ladies" (1886) refutes the imputation of wholesale sentimentality to Miss Jewett's work. This memorial to two old sisters' misadventures in time and place contains the sharpest satire of which she is capable. It is found in the allegorical nomenclature (Dulham, Dobin, Greenaples, Hightree, Clovenfoot), in the viewpoints of younger villagers and the French salesman, in the superabundance of verbal obliquities. No page is without its little sting.

The basic theme was enunciated by Robert Burns upon seeing a louse on a lady's bonnet (one has to smile at the closeness of this instigation and the Misses Dobins' hairpieces):

> O wad some Power the giftie gie us
> To see oursels as ithers see us!

The sisters Dobin decide to acquire artificial frizettes to counteract the onslaught of baldness. They travel to a nearby town, are duped into buying preposterously outmoded bangs, and return ecstatic, ready to astound Dulham society with their fashionable new adornments.

Two tributary techniques feed the major purpose—contrasts of past–present and country–city. The Dobins are so devotedly attached to the historic glory of family and town that they fail to keep pace with changing mores. They behave as though the old hierarchies still prevail and as if they occupy the highest brackets. But the falling out of their hair indicates the relentless passage of time, and their failure to adapt is demonstrated by the fatigue they immediately feel after discovering that their father's friend has gone out of business and they must venture into the newer, unfamiliar shops.

Miss Jewett is not so sympathetic with their situation as with that of Dan'el Gunn. In "An Autumn Holiday" the entire village accepts and protects the deluded old man. Some elder contemporaries in Dulham are humanely dismayed over this foolishness of the dear old ladies, but the new people and the younger generation deride them unmercifully. The stance of these newcomers and youngsters, in fact, constitutes the chief vantage from which the reader sees the Dobins. These country innocents go to Westbury, "a consequential manufacturing town," and are confused and victimized in a way far more shameful than the Pinkhams in "Fame's Little Day." Particularly villainous is the cynical Frenchman, embodiment of the shoddy values of the present and the drive for material gain whatever the cost in personal probity.

Miss Jewett draws a stronger line between the intrinsic pathos of the antiquarian sisters and the necessity to adjust to altering norms. She favors the modern perspective, and from the bite of her ironies one would think that she has momentarily lost patience with retrogressive old ladies. And perhaps she has. Her tone is not so "gentle" or "tender" as has been described. A sentimental realist, she understands that there are two sides to be considered. She selects her governing symbol with rare discrimination; it is a wax model in the shop window which smiles at the sisters as they enter but which turns out to be "plain plaster of Paris" when looked at from the rear. When they leave, Lucinda is hypocritically granted "a last smile from the handsome wax countenance." For skill of organization, subtlety of characterization, and sensitivity to ethos, this story must be rated among Miss Jewett's truly memorable accomplishments. However, one hesitates to say with Aldrich "that Hawthorne's pallid allegories will have faded away long before those two little Dulham ladies."[11]

Speaking of Hawthorne brings up the elderly sisters Betsey and Hannah Knowles, two suppressed, isolated spinsters who find that their miserly father has left a fortune ("In Dark New England Days," 1890). This means freedom finally to live as they had never been allowed to in his lifetime. Robbed of the legacy, Hannah utters a frightful curse upon the suspected thief and his descendants in a scene dramatically enhanced by the fact that she is far less aggressive than her sister. Pity is evoked by their demolished hopes, but the latent power in the situation is never fully realized. The intensity of the crucial scene peters out indeterminately. Miss Jewett's recourse to italics and to the eye at the window briefly conjures up Poe's "The Tell-Tale Heart."

IX *The Younger Folk*

Miss Jewett treats less frequently with the younger generations in Maine, and usually in some relation or comparison with their forebears. She contemplates the general exodus of youngsters to the cities or to the expanding West. She presents occasional youngsters who continue the old traditions with considerably more zeal than their immediate predecessors. She depicts the destructive despotism of the past and the arrant ingratitudes of youth. Mostly she is perturbed by the indifference to ancestral ideals and by a coarsened moral texture.

"By the Morning Boat" (1890) records the ritualistic preliminaries to a country boy's baptism in the larger world. In a procession of encounters he takes leave of his grandfather, mother, sister, and two neighbors. Out of these junctures flashes the quality of the natives' pride and reluctance to see him leave the land, and the boy's eagerness to test wider horizons. Elisha is one of Miss Jewett's brightest young people; at fifteen he is the man of the house since his father is dead and his grandfather is an enfeebled old seaman. His is also the eternal aspiration of youth for space and chance. Elisha, aching to try his mettle in the new conditions of commercial Boston, is full of Horatio Alger-like plans "for coming home, rich and generous enough to make [his mother] proud and happy." He boards the steamer in a tremor of excitement, scorning the suggestion that he might be going only as far as Bath. As moments lengthen, he exults in the possession of his own power of direction and responsibility. Like all classic young heroes who make the clean break, he is at last "alone, but unfettered and aflame with courage."

Miss Jewett employs symbols with exquisite aptness. The boat is a Viking vehicle for the long journey. It is morning, the beginning of a new day as this is the beginning of Elisha's new life. Boston is the full leap into the world, not the halfway measure Bath would be. Old Mrs. Stover, who significantly is bedridden, gives him a watch which is the heritage of time passing from age to youth. The caged woodchuck which Elisha releases before his departure is representative of his own freed self, just as the frightened squirrel mimics Henry Fleming in *The Red Badge of Courage* or the turtle symbolizes mankind in *The Grapes of Wrath*.

Andrew Phillips of "Andrew's Fortune" (1881) does not have the initial grit of young Elisha. An irresolute "book fool," he is willing to wait around while hoping that events will turn out instead of trying to mould them to his benefit. Propelled by circumstances, he goes to Boston, takes to business, and makes a fortune—a projection, as it were, of Elisha's future. To fortify Andrew, Miss Jewett brings in Dunning, who functions as forecast and channel for Andrew's action. Dunning is a native who went to Boston as a boy, became wealthy, and now gives Andrew his first opportunity. He might be seen as the impersonation of fate if Miss Jewett did not make clear that Andrew's fate comes in the shape of "the hand of God." The story is built speciously around a lost will and a late retrieval, but it rests on the small-town-boy-makes-good-in-the-big-city theme. This time Miss Jewett intimates that success comes easier from commerce than from the land.

"The Mate of the Daylight" (1882) is a quizzical success story which thrusts handsome but unstable Daniel Lewis into unfavorable contrast with three retired sea captains. He has done little to recommend himself insofar as work is concerned ("Dan'l al'ays was all talk and no cider"), and he seems to woo Captain Ryder's granddaughter less for love than for her anticipated legacy. By an improbable turnabout, he takes command of a vessel in an emergency, settles down to his occupation, marries Susan, and is all set for a life commendable to the critical captains. The balancing of past and present factors is patent; for, through his ultimate acceptance of command and responsibility, Lewis falls in line with the work morality of older generations of New Englanders.

But the reader does not get to know him well enough to credit or discredit his amazing reversal of attitude. Rather than being a chip off the old cod, he appears an opportunist who sees the main chance and grabs it; in the case of the ship, estimably; in the case of the girl, equivocally. Again Miss Jewett puts the new hero in question; this modern version of the sea captain succeeds, but his primary impetus is monetary gain, not the romance of shipping out. The three antiquated captains are more substantially drawn; and—tough, dedicated, inquisitive, narrow-minded, and scintillating talkers—they arrogate attention from the feeble narrative.

Warren Price of "An Only Son" (1883) is another young man who after heavy trials makes the best of his capacities. His secrecy brings him under temporary suspicion of robbing his father. When the curtain is completely lifted, he steps forward as an honest, ingenious son of the soil. This story recapitulates Miss Jewett's creed about the two-sidedness of human nature and events: "There are some people who are like the moon," she says, "always with one side hidden and turned away." One should see both sides before forming an opinion.

When Miss Jewett creates an absolute young hero, it generally turns out to be a young heroine. Polly Finch is the brawniest of the lot. When her aging father breaks down and cries over the progressive worsening of his situation, Polly puts aside further

thought of teaching, seizes hold of the farm, and brings it gradually back to a sound basis. A true Demeter, she repairs her
father's shattered morale and the family finances so well that,
before the story ends, she has earned the appellation she covets,
Farmer Finch. When life threatens to flicker out, she guards it
grimly, for it is her talent to live. She "made up her mind to be
son and daughter both"; in fact, she becomes a better man than
her father and her lover.

Although a psychiatric study might be made of Miss Jewett's
penchant for transforming sexes—Dan'el Gunn, Ann Floyd, Polly
Finch, Mrs. Mary Wilson, and others—that is beyond the present
scope. Two matters in "Farmer Finch" (1885), however, call for
comment—a structural and a symbolic effect which invigorate
the narrative impact. As the story opens, John Finch, in low
spirits, is approaching his farm from one direction while Polly,
equally depressed, is approaching the farm from another direction; both converge with bad news upon the third member of
the family, Mrs. Finch, "tired and hungry and almost frightened."
The resultant scene touches the depth of their accumulated
misfortunes.

The ruling symbol is a barberry bush which Polly notices as
she is walking home. The berries look gray, dry, and spoiled
when she nears them; but, when she examines them from the
other side, they are glowing like rubies. "There are two ways of
looking at more things than barberry bushes," she decides. When
her circumstance is most troublesome, she falls back on this con-
solation: "I'll see if the other side is any better, like my barberry bush." Upon the frame of this analogy Miss Jewett weaves
the theme that innate talent (farming) supersedes acquired
training (teaching), another sanction for the natural and against
the contrived.

In "The Life of Nancy" (1895), Nancy Gale's body is disabled
but her spirit is as puissant as Polly's. She is so pointedly the
self-effacing humanitarian that some of the sympathy a reader
feels in the irony of her lively nature entombed in handicapped
flesh is lost in the almost maudlin pathos; Nancy is just too
good. Nevertheless, the story has some noteworthy touches. It
is one of the few stories in which the city and its people do not
come off black in comparison to countryfolk and their ways. It
displays the intrinsic self-sufficiency of natives through the old
farmer who "goes his way alike unconscious of seeing or being

seen" and through "how little compassion for Nancy these country neighbors expressed." It strikes another blow for conservation of Maine's natural resources. It attributes to "the curious insistence of fate" the city hero's recurrent involvement in Nancy's existence. And its mention of Rip Van Winkle betokens Washington Irving's influence on Miss Jewett's essays.

"The King of Folly Island" (1886) involves a monomaniac who vows he will not set foot on anyone's land but his own, and it portrays the blighting effect of this oath on his daughter. It contains the ingredients and potential for tragedy, which it fails to achieve because Miss Jewett has not the desire nor the temperament to keep Quint's ferocious pride or his daughter Phebe's terrible affliction in paramount view. The emphasis shifts with diminishing conviction from the mad "King" to John Frankfort, the vacationing businessman, and it is also sometimes divided between Phebe and her similarly doomed mother. It is nonetheless one of Miss Jewett's flintiest stories.

The main line of narrative traces the "King's" relations with his daughter. As a result of his oath Phebe, who has affected lungs, is veritably imprisoned and sentenced to death on this otherwise uninhabited island. A secondary line intertwines Frankfort's subjective misgivings, a country–city contrast, and a perspective from the outside. In the end Miss Jewett certifies that human beings are fundamentally of the same stripe regardless of environment or experience. Egocentricity, whether it occurs in a trawler or a tycoon, is reprehensible. For Frankfort soon realizes he too is a king of Folly Island. He too has isolated himself from humanity through his obsession to amass as much money as possible. The difference between him and George Quint is that Frankfort learns in time that no man is an island, and he begins to rectify his error. The "King" persists in his folly without recognition or abatement. For one brief moment the city again is ascendant.

The point of view is that of city eyes surveying country ways. Some of these, in danger of being ignored because too familiar or ingrained, are caught in a fresh aspect by alert, alien Frankfort. Miss Jewett presents the quarrels, the biases, the superstitions, the shortcomings, the skullduggeries, the pettiness of insulated and uneducated natives as seen for the first time, although she is recording them for perhaps the thousandth. For the most part they emerge from dialogue, without special lighting or editorial comment. The dismal tale is appropriately played out in an atmosphere of barnacled timbers, useless boats, empty barrels, broken lobster pots, and miscellaneous litter, all slowly decomposing in the relentless weather. "Go on dreaming about the world; that is better," says Frankfort to Phebe, and undoubtedly it was. Like Eugene O'Neill's terrified barflies, only through illusion can she tolerate the appalling reality of living.

The text of "A Landless Farmer" (1883) is equally universal. In it the younger generation vividly illustrates man's inhumanity to man, and Miss Jewett makes no effort to disguise her two sources, King Lear and the Prodigal Son. This cheerless chronicle —two ingrate daughters mistreat their ill and aged father until he is rescued by his son who returns after long absence—is developed too leisurely to succeed entirely in its purpose. It also suffers from a prolonged, pendant explanation. Compensatory excellence resides in Miss Jewett's continued devotion to detail and in her characterizations of Serena, a miscreant and shrew; of skulking, miserly Aaron; of inept Mary, the malingerer; and of Ezra Allen, the voice of decency.

"The Hiltons' Holiday" (1893) is in effect the induction of the newest generation to the wonders of the world and to the dignity of tradition. All the tribal mores are observed. The mother remains home while the father escorts his two little girls in the cyclical journey from farm to town and back to the soil, with a votive gift for the matriarch. Tired and happy, the children go to bed. The parents linger a moment outside, looking over the shadowy fields in silent communion. "The great day was over, and they shut the door." The mood of a race epic is attained.

All four principals are important to the evolution of this symbolic day, but incident becomes illustrative mainly through the neatly drafted progress of the girls' paired reactions. Katy, the soberer of the two, is more appreciative of the beauty and the meaning of the past. Her frequently noted resemblance to her father's mother confirms her affinity with older days; of the two, she will be the perpetuator of the past. Susan is less impressed by time-consuming reminiscences and by Judge Masterson, the emblem of bygone erudition and gentility. She delights in having her picture taken and in mixing with the passing scene. Katy and Susan are fundamental figures who represent the deferential and the indifferent postures toward history and ancestry that Miss Jewett dramatizes in so much of her work.

This vignette of contentment turns up the other side of the coin of New England life. No especial poverty or controversy is visible in it. Some trivial bickering usual in family intercourse occurs, but a controlled tone of excitement in an atmosphere of over-all felicity prevails. The utter simplicity of presentation accords with nearness to earth and celebration of homely values.

X *Return of the Natives*

Natives who return to Maine after an absence of several decades are useful to Miss Jewett as instruments not only for comparison of past–present and youth–age but also for study of the effects of experience in the outside world. The great allure of fame and of wealth, of the cities and of the West, which plundered Maine of its most enterprising youths in the middle 1800's was a sore point with Miss Jewett. On the whole, her emigrés gain pelf but lose their souls. In the major stories based on this pattern of departure and return only one character, a woman, turns out the better for having been away.

When Rebecca Parsons comes back after living forty years in various western parishes with her brother, fear of change impels her to preserve her illusions of Brookfield as it had been when she left. Fortunately, she is made much of by some cousins when she arrives. She also meets and marries the recently bereaved minister after a short courtship. The story subsides on a note of God's infinite providence, the wonderfully connected ramifications of His plan. The social consequences of "Miss Becky's Pilgrimage" (1881), however, lie in such mundane matters as the amusement of youth over the pursuit and marriage of elderly Rebecca, the crime of railroads in supplanting waterways as media of travel and occupation, the division of interest between East and West, and the pathos of old women who cannot see themselves as others see them.

"A New Parishioner" (1883) is stronger in texture and characterization. Reputedly wealthy, Henry Stroud returns to his home town and bestows many benefactions upon individuals, church, and community. He endears himself to all but Lydia Dunn, who, because she cannot shake off the feeling that there is something illicit about him, resists his attentions. It transpires that he has led a crooked life and that his "gifts" are paid for with worthless notes. Lydia's reputation for astuteness soars when she is revealed as the only one who was right about Henry.

Lydia accepts the public verdict of superior discretion but suffers private realization of how narrow the actual margin is between being right and being wrong. Despite her instinctive distrust of Henry, she had dallied momentarily with the possibility of matrimony. With rare discursive artistry, Miss Jewett forecasts this internal incertitude through the play on black and white and gray cats. Two other characters who function prominently are the craven clergyman, etched deeply and broadly, and Jonas Phipps, the home-grown interlocutor who balances Henry Stroud. Like Ezra Allen in "A Landless Farmer," Jonas provides the inside view; reacting with typical intensity or unconcern to the situation, he describes it in aboriginal idiom, with a native touch of color.

Best in this return-of-the-native category is "A Native of Winby" (1891), in which the protagonist is most keenly and continuously scrutinized. The Honorable Joseph K. Laneway, a general, senator, and millionaire, takes a sentimental journey to the humble village of his birth. He has long dreamed of the adulation he will receive on this occasion; instead, he is given short shrift by many who neither remember him nor know of his present eminence. At the point of bleakest discouragement, he stops at the house of Abby Hender, his first sweetheart. He expands out of his misery when she greets him as "Joe Laneway, *you same boy!*" She reminisces pleasantly and prepares some of his favorite dishes as he vividly relives his childhood days. After an altogether satisfying visit, he departs in a glow. At the railroad station he is honored ostentatiously by a large group of citizens.

Laneway's tension exists in his dual capacity for civic and domestic values. He craves recognition for his accomplishments, yet he wishes to retrieve the radiance of youth. The inner man is sated by Mrs. Hender's restoration of his boyhood; the outer man is appeased by the political attention at the station. Which is the true Laneway—the man looking for applause or the man looking for the boy? The gist of his ambivalence lies in two of Mrs. Hender's quiet remarks. "I'm real glad they showed him proper respect," and, "I had the best part of anybody."

Laneway has come to prefer the outward show first, while

not forgetting original worth. Mrs. Hender admits the need of the former, then puts her finger on the heart of the matter. This story is Miss Jewett's comment on two stalwart natives: the man who left and the woman who stayed. Both retain the hard-won ideals of the region. Laneway's are somewhat bruised and disfigured by the enervating demands of a hustling world. Mrs. Hender's remain steadfast and untarnished in the quiet seclusion of the country.

XI *Holiday Stories*

Miss Jewett wrote numerous occasional stories, mostly about Christmas and Thanksgiving, some about Easter and New Year's Day. These were often solicited by editors or were produced by Miss Jewett with obvious aim at holiday issues of newspapers or magazines; and none can be ranked with her hardier stock. "A Neighbor's Landmark" and "Law Lane" conclude on Christmas, and "Aunt Cynthy Dallett" on New Year's Day, but these are incidental fillips in stories with stronger supporting themes. *An Empty Purse*, "Mary and Martha," and "The Night Before Thanksgiving"—tightly hitched to the days they celebrate—can be lauded for little beyond Miss Jewett's dependable style and her insights into feminine character. An overplus of sentiment mars all of them. In the first story, Debby Gaines enacts the adage that giving is more important than the gift; the second and third exemplify the biblical verse "Cast thy bread upon the waters: for thou shalt find it after many days," and are resolved by opportune deliverances.

"Decoration Day" (1892) is the most adequate of the occasional tales. Miss Jewett lavishes pathos on the war veterans ravaged by time and civic hostility, but she escapes sentimentality through sheer virtuosity of art. The parade, with one crippled soldier riding in a cart, wends through town, the outlying area, and the cemetery. Its melancholic splendor gradually dissipates the resentment of the community and brings it to full appreciation of the services these men had once rendered their country. The magic is not in this revival of patriotic ardor but in the more subtle and wider-based emotion it leads to. By an exquisite transferral which occurs without awareness in most of the spectators, they are suffused with sympathy for their less fortunate fellows; they pass from superficial approval to intense subjective love.

As a result, animosity and disdain are forgotten. The failures of these motley old marchers are put aside as they are honored for rising to glory in the crucible of war. In the long routine of daily existence most of them went under, lacking either the merits of mediocrity demanded of "good citizens" or the stamina to live through the twenty-four hours of a day without the martial urgencies of survival, courage, challenge, or comradeship in arms to sustain them. The gallant procession forges the disgruntled community into a magnetic chain of humanity. With one dramatic and pathetic spectacle the old soldiers restore the balance of a town that had overlooked its debt and underestimated its endowment. Dignity and self-respect return to both the critics and the criticized.

XII *Business, Foreigners, and the South*

Three other classifications of short stories should be mentioned, if only briefly, in any review of Miss Jewett's work: those about business, those about Irish and French-Canadian immigrants, and those about the South. In none of these is she at crest, for she loses pungency and firmness whenever she invades extrinsic territories. Only in the third group does she approximate the substance of her native inspiration.

She knew more about business and commerce than Parrington is willing to concede. Left in comfortable financial circumstances, she nevertheless manipulated the income from her writing and investments with uncommon sharpness. She learned enough about the economics of production and distribution, and of management and dividends to imbue her stories in this area with a film of authenticity. She is neither reformer nor muckraker. She sees the evils of the industrial system but inclines to commiserate with single souls caught in its advance rather than attack the force that is producing an unwanted new order. She clucks politely at the emergent plutocracy and its sycophantic urban middle class, "those who have no inherited sense or discretion in the use of money."[12] The caste she was born and bred in was still securely above that kind of vulgarity. Implicit in all these stories is the superiority of the old over the new, the country over the city.

"Tom's Husband" (1882) is meant to amuse by its husband–wife transposition—Tom Wilson takes care of the house and his wife runs the business. Miss Jewett also makes it a repository for sundry observations about changing conditions in New England. The refusal of natives to man the new factories and the Irish trend westward necessitate importation of French-Canadians. Tom's laming by machinery symbolizes the dangers of this mechanical way of life to the younger generations. Women entering business in growing numbers do so to the detriment of their "womanliness." The surprisingly anti-feminist dénouement leaves no doubt about Miss Jewett's conservatism. With only slight obeisance to the repressive effects of convention upon enterprising females, she declares it fitting that—away from the soil—a man be a man, a woman a woman.

Similarly frivolous is the plot of "The Two Browns" (1886), which depends upon successful maintenance of duple identity. J. Benedict Brown, a lawyer-aristocrat, stoops to commerce under a thin alias, becomes proud of his money-making prowess, but defects quickly when exposure seems imminent. The preferability of a profession over a trade is asserted in the difference between the shining brass doorplate on Brown's Broadway law office and the fly-by-night atmosphere of his Ninth Avenue business establishment. Characters are shallow and typical. The story is notable only for Miss Jewett's display of knowledge about the actualities of everyday business, of the wiles of promotion and selling.

In restless semi-retirement, John Craven of "A Business Man" (1886) comes to the realization that money isn't everything. He attempts to redeem his neglect of human values by supplying capital for an ambitious, impecunious young man. Before he dies, Craven has the satisfaction of seeing his protégé happily married and prospering. In "A Business Man" this theme of the poor rich man is somberly edifying and less imaginatively treated than in "The King of Folly Island."

Two stories deal with the ruthless disregard of individual welfare by machine morality. "The Failure of David Berry" (1891) records the bewildering pressures brought to bear on a humane, capable artisan by a flood of ready-made factory goods. He is forced out of his pleasant home workshop by shifts in the tide of trade, into symbolically dark and narrow quarters in town, then into unmanageable debt. David Berry's failure is that of the old individualism to understand or accept the new mechanism. Like Billy Budd, who also faced an enigmatic force, Berry's triumph comes in death, not life.

"The Gray Mills of Farley" (1898) offers every provocation for an arraignment of big business and its mistreatment of small people, but Miss Jewett again chooses to probe the personal predicament instead of the social or moral implications. She notes the rapacity of directors who shut down a factory because they are more intent upon dividends than the fate of workers. With unaccustomed asperity she scores the congenital antagonisms between capital and labor, and she decries the hunger and helplessness brought on by economic dislocation. Her final response to these conditions, however, is romantic. The native company agent, the priest, and the factory hands resort to primitive mutual aid while hoping for the mill to reopen. Miraculously, it resumes operation before they all move away or starve. Life recommences its former pace, as though no one has been hurt. Miss Jewett's only retort to industrial exploitation is Christian communism.

Miss Jewett, who liked what she saw in immigrant Irish and French-Canadians, wished to give them "a more true and sympathetic rendering" than those of stage caricaturists and local-color zealots. She found these new settlers industrious, loyal, ebullient, sensitive, tough, and devout. She knew what pains of strangeness and insecurity they suffered, and she blamed the cheapening standards of America when they went wrong. But sympathy was not enough to produce truth, and her immigrants miss the distinctive solidity of her New England natives. They speak violent and brilliant dialects, behave in abrupt and volatile patterns. Ironically, they exhibit precisely the exaggerated qualities she deplores in so much New England local-color literature.

"The Luck of the Bogans" (1889) is a dramatic paradox in which liquor, the source of Mike Bogan's material wealth, is also the cause of his son's moral ruin. Miss Jewett makes of this situation a combined temperance lecture and vaudeville. There have doubtless existed viragos like Peggy Muldoon, but Miss Jewett crams several of the most raffish into one unforgettable explosion. The least affected action is Mike's destruction of his grogshop in an agonized, instinctive rage against fate after the death of his son.

Another Irish lad who comes to no good among American snares is Dan Nolan, sick in body as well as soul. Miss Jewett's profound respect for the Catholic priesthood appears in Father

Ryan's near-impossible conversion of this bad lot. "Between Mass and Vespers" (1893) goes behind the scenes of a man of God's extraordinary service to humanity during what appears an ordinary day of scheduled rituals. The theology of turning the other cheek consummates a rehabilitation where dogma and force fail.

To show that the Irish dream can be fulfilled on alien soil, Miss Jewett implements some of her stories with highly personable, euphoric colleens who bend circumstances to their needs. "A Little Captive Maid" (1891) retells the tale of Naaman and the Israelite slave, substituting America for Syria and Ireland for Samaria. Nora Connelly rejuvenates Captain Balfour and is rewarded with enough money to return to Ireland, marry, and circumvent her unkind aunt. "Where's Nora" (1898) also portrays America as the pot at rainbow's end which is to be ransacked and left to rust. There is no sentiment except for Ireland. The goal is to acquire a sufficient bank account to enable one to return. In this conventional paradigm, Nora combines the American success story and the triumphant return to the old country and family. The impression is left that an interval in America is tantamount to a descent to Hades.

Miss Jewett falls short again in "Bold Words at the Bridge" (1899) in which she trades in surface qualities and fanciful dialogue. She attempts to do with two irate Irishwomen what she so often does splendidly with two Maine matrons, but the tone and effects are strained. The strident quarrelers are "quaint" and oversimplified.

The French-Canadians Miss Jewett describes are from the same peasant class as the immigrant Irish. "Mère Pochette" (1888), a long and pointlessly ironical narrative, is distinguished by a superb sketch of the protagonist, a tightfisted, self-reliant, contemptuous, ignorant, bold, foxy, and remorseless widow who is determined to have her way, by fair means or foul. The flow of xenophobia in this story is reversed in "Little French Mary" (1895). The lovely manners and cheerful disposition of this child dissolve all feelings of native resentment, and when she must move back to Canada, regret is wholesale. In the unswervable widow and captivating child Miss Jewett epitomizes traits of toughness and tenderness she openly admires in this vigorous race from the North. Once more, however, the fault is that of too meager acquaintance.

Some mystic kinship of misfortune gave Miss Jewett securer linkage to character and conditions in the South. Her aristocratic sensibility could understand the encroachments made on plantation society by the Civil War and the Reconstruction Era, just as it could understand the impact made on the captains and dowagers of rural New England by the Embargo and the railroads. Concentrating on luckless post-bellum patricians, she produced stories about the South incomparably better than those about Irish and French-Canadian commonfolk.

"The Mistress of Sydenham Plantation" (1888) leads Miss Jewett's Southern studies. Mistress Sydenham is a counterpart of Deephaven's Miss Chauncey, with the added tragedy of displacement by war. A hallucinated relic who has lost all her property and most of her faculties, she orders her one remaining servitor to take her on a tour of her "estate." He goes through a travesty of inspecting the old place, which has been confiscated and turned into farms for former slaves. At the end of a humiliating ride in a broken-down cart, they come into view of the crumbled mansion, so reminiscent of the abandoned farms in York County. The Mistress stares impassively into space, as though present reality is more than she wishes to face. The vision of a glorious past gleams at her from another level. In this allegory of the South's shattered grandeur, nostalgia and neurotic pride have induced fantasy. Many of Miss Jewett's New England motifs are recognizable here, supported by purposive details of landscape and psychology. She is at home in this confluence of dignity and degradation. One feels the strength and confidence of her finest style again.

Tom Burton of Boston and Colonel Bellamy of Virginia incarnate their respective regions in the North–South confrontation that energizes "A War Debt" (1895). The impoverished Colonel is punctilious about keeping up manorial appearances before the young stranger who has come to restore a family souvenir pillaged during the war. Tom quickly realizes the calamitous straits this once-exalted family is in and sympathy of class for class transcends sectional animosities. He impulsively gives his gun to the Colonel, a figurative renewal of trust between victor and vanquished. Tom also vows to return, for he hopes for a romance with the beautiful granddaughter he has glimpsed on the train. The reunion of tragically split North and South will be brought about not by restrictive laws and military police but by the gentle hands of superior culture reaching for each other through a haze of political strife. Miss Jewett's descriptions of the run-down plantation with the Spartan Colonel and his lame consort in the foreground, the pathetically skimpy supper, and the irresponsibly merry ex-slaves, are as sensitive and appreciative as her reports on Dulham society.

In Miss Jewett's short stories subsist all the characters and themes for which she is justly esteemed in *Deephaven* and *The Country of the Pointed Firs*. The short stories allowed her many fresh opportunities to diversify and deepen her favored subject matter. From "Jenny Garrow's Lovers" (1868) to "A Spring Sunday" (1904) she presents an infinitude of variations, all contributing to the composite Down East spirit she re-created more vitally than any of her contemporaries. Her stories seldom comply wholly with the predilections of magazine editors. By 1875 she had evolved a comfortable compromise between her digressive temperament and the tailored techniques of conventional short stories. Within this self-legislated leeway she carved out for herself an enviable place in enduring American fiction of the nineteenth century.

CHAPTER 6

The Country of the Sad Captains

LONG BEFORE she attempted to write a novel, Miss Jewett knew the genre was incongruous to her aptitudes. In 1873 she wrote Scudder: "I have no dramatic talent. . . . It seems to me I can furnish the theatre, and show you the actors, and the scenery, and the audience, but there never is any play!"[1] There is, of course, no universally accepted definition of the novel, but it is generally granted that it should contain a modicum of physical or psychological action, some intricacy of plot which carries the characters through to a significant qualitative change. As opposed to the short story, which *reveals* through instantaneous flashes, the novel *develops* through continuous accruals. It must be said, then, that Miss Jewett's fame rests on a form which may be called the paranovel. *Deephaven* and *The Country of the Pointed Firs* lack important elements customarily expected in a novel. Although *A Country Doctor, A Marsh Island,* and *The Tory Lover* come closer to the ordinary concept of the novel, they may hardly be listed among her auspicious flights.

In all but the last of these Miss Jewett concentrates on place and people to the exclusion of dynamic action. But Thompson wisely observes that elaborate incident "in the case of quiet country life, introduces an element of improbability" and would convey "a distorted aspect of strenuous liveliness" which her domain does not possess.[2] Through irreproachable details of landscape and interior she creates a solid background against which she sets unique personalities working out their destinies in unspectacular routines. She had the genius to perceive the slight but signal object, shade, and gesture, and to put them in telling perspective. She is less concerned with finicky organization of event than she is with a dusty escritoire, a herb remedy, or a frown on the face of a passing native. She avoids frenzied interconnections between her characters, but she pries sensitively into the hidden internal worlds of each. She does not grapple with the big issues, nor does she make much of the grand passion.

Other novelists may capture the imagination of readers with stir and involvement; Miss Jewett does it by complete dominion over tone and point of view. She achieves the temper of a soft autumnal afternoon, not the heat of midsummer or the rush of a winter gale. Her novels do not attract the audience that more incisive or vehement volumes do, but Whittier attests the love they inspire: "When tired and worried I resort to thy books and find rest and refreshing. I recommend them to everybody, and everybody likes them. There is no dissenting opinion."[3]

In her 1893 Preface to *Deephaven*, Miss Jewett reviews the reasons that impelled her to write about her own region. The Civil War, railroads, immigration, summer visitors, and the exodus of young natives effected extraordinary changes in rustic life. She felt obliged to honor Plato's dictum that "the best thing that can be done for the people of a state is to make them acquainted with one another." The diminution of respect for old customs and culture, the frivolous alteration of traditional architecture, and the loss of individuality made it urgent to reanimate the values of the hallowed past for the heedless present. To help city and country folk understand each other, and to expose the current age to the finest ideals of expired or expiring generations—in one or the other of these respects, this is what all her novels are about.

I *Deephaven*

The first chapters of Harriet Beecher Stowe's *The Pearl of Orr's Island*, which Miss Jewett read when about fourteen, helped her "to see with new eyes" the decaying, shipless harbors of Maine and the shore paths that led from one weatherbeaten house to another. The first section of *Deephaven* appeared in the *Atlantic Monthly* in 1873. By 1877 Howells had convinced the young author to collect other related sketches, provide suitable continuity, and publish them as a novel. The favorable reception by most critics and the public was a satisfaction to Miss Jewett, who seemed principally interested in knowing if the royalties would be enough for the purchase of "a most gallant new horse."[4]

An interesting correlative exists in the fact that *Deephaven* appeared in the same year (1877) as James's *The American.* Both books contain the writers' seminal ideas and methods, early workings out of style, situations, characters, and themes that were later to be developed and consolidated with unerring distinction. As James must have been trying to write *The Ambassadors,* so Miss Jewett must have been trying to write *The Country of the Pointed Firs.* Both lacked the experience, the maturity necessary for the subtler execution. Scores of novelists, from Fielding through Joyce, have returned reinforced to a youthful conception. After almost twenty years Miss Jewett sublimated *Deephaven* in *The Country of the Pointed Firs. Deephaven* has indubitable merit but, as Willa Cather and numerous others point out, it is "a beginning raw work,"[5] a product whose sporadic excellence requires the firming hand of time for fullest realization.

No coherent action regulates the several elements. A simulated unity is obtained through the ubiquitous presence of Helen Denis and Kate Lancaster, two city girls who come to stay for a summer in the home of the latter's deceased grandaunt, Katherine Brandon. Their activities are tidily bounded in the first chapter by their preparations and arrival and in the last chapter by their reminiscences and departure. In between occurs a disjointed pattern of events, not entirely chronological. "Brandon House" serves as a focus from which the girls fare in search of novelty: they visit the lighthouse, the burying-ground, a church service; take high tea with a social lion; see the decrepit wharves and fishhouses, various farms; attend a circus, a lecture, a funeral; go to another village. They ride, walk through the woods, go fishing, berrying and mushrooming; they talk to the widows, the spinsters, the captains, the minister. No characteristic of environment or society is overlooked; and out of this welter of picaresque movement between places and persons emerges an exhaustive biography of Deephaven terrain, traditions, and populace.

"Brandon House" has value not only as a symbol of past grandeur but also as a functional point of view. Miss Jewett's world embraces the sea and the woods, the port and the farm. In many of her sketches and short stories she takes a stance from which she can watch and describe both. From the landing of "Brandon House" may be seen the hills far inland; from an upper hall window, the sea. For expressive point of view, how-

ever, one must examine the two summer visitors, Helen and
Kate, who are the eyes and minds through which Deephaven
unfolds. They have the advantage of coming freshly and reacting
originally to an unfamiliar community. The local plight is more
apparent to them, for it contrasts sharply with the urban, Brahmin surroundings to which they are accustomed. Genuinely
sympathetic and interested, they meet people on their own
ground, win their confidence, and make them want to talk. Kate,
who is less reticent, acts the provocative primer and keeps informative monologues from languishing. She can be diplomatic,
too, changing the subject when Danny shows embarrassment
over his disclosures.

But they are far from perfect crystals. Both are twenty-four
but confess to behaving like girls six or seven years old—desiring
to play in boats, build sand castles, and carry dolls. They resist
becoming "irreparably grown-up" and constantly pursue excitement. Once they eavesdrop behind a warehouse while the
captains are conversing. They deny sentimentality yet write a
tragic journal on antique yellow letter paper; they deny con-
descension yet think of themselves as embarking on a privileged
lark (Kate writes to Helen of the plan "in which you and I are
chief characters"). Worst of all, Miss Jewett uses them un-
blushingly as automatic megaphones for her own soliloquies.
Helen narrates in an informal, though not familiar, manner, as
if talking to an uninvolved spectator over her shoulder while in
full tilt with the experience. Thus it comes as something of a
shock when she turns squarely around and lapses into stilted
rhetoric and owlish cogitation. Often she supplies aspects of
background and character not apparent in an interchange. Helen
and Kate hold deftly organized discussions on eschatology and
related topics. The book closes after their summary of the charms
of country life and their solemn happiness in having sampled
them. The girls are vested with separate bodies and personalities
but they are really the didactic, compulsively childlike alter
ego of Sarah Orne Jewett.

These characteristics, however, end the maladroitness of *Deephaven,* and they are flaws that may be laid to the young author's
clumsiness with her tools. The materials themselves she arrayed
with sure skill, evoking through place, people, and customs the
genius immanent in this special world, the mood of memory and
peace that envelops it. Deephaven is as real to her as Berwick

or York but she will not identify it as a particular place; it is not to be found on the map of New England. Deephaven is in fact the essence of her observation and imagination.

The village is becomingly isolated in space and time. It stands at the edge of the ocean, some dozen miles from the railroad. It is utterly out of fashion and more or less out of repair. The clocks seem to have stopped long ago and everything with them. Schooners and brigs slowly disintegrate along inactive wharves, while warehouses lean and finally fall. The bordering farm area is no less quiescent.

Miss Jewett's supreme consideration is people, viewed individually and as a group by her two eager young aristocrats. The society is predominantly matriarchal. Women outnumber the men and are the more robust. Men are largely reduced to idleness and take refuge in various stratagems to avoid admitting their impotence. Many of the captains achieve their title by brevet on passing a proper age. Chronically rheumatic, they spend their days recalling past glamor. Mrs. Kew's nephew is a guileless youth at forty; Dick Carew hides in the library; the wretched farmer of "In Shadow" succumbs to drink when his wife dies.

The old outnumber the young, who have fled the discouraging soil to work in shops and factories. Miss Jewett herself points out the irony of the lecture on Elements of True Manhood—"it was directed entirely toward young men, and there was not a young man there." Remnants of strength may be seen in the dispassionate acceptance of nature's laws by the common folk and in the stately dependence of the eldest generation upon ancestry and tradition.

Solidarity resides in the ingrained observance of social gradations, clearly defined in the chapter "Deephaven Society." All members of this tacitly stratified community remember with "far more deference than is consistent with the principles of republican government" the grand status of extinct Governor Chantrey, who kept a valet, sported a coach, and gave regal entertainments in the mansion which is now only a cellar. Contemporary society consists of three distinguishable levels: the gentry, represented by such as Honora Carew, Miss Chauncey, and Katharine Brandon; the middle class, by Mr. Dockum, Mrs. Kew, the questionable Widow Tully, and all the sad captains; the lower order, by Danny, the stricken farmer's family, Mrs. Bonny. The amalgam of this society is good manners; the link between upper and lower castes, *noblesse oblige*. Current nobility is wary of intrusive forces that may undermine its entrenched position. Miss Carew cannot feel too grateful that "there was no disagreeable foreign population."

Miss Jewett's capacity for suggesting the norm by presenting multiple facets of the unusual is abundantly evident here. Dignity, self-sufficiency, self-respect, fellow-feeling, and reverence are demonstrated through a gallery of vivid personalities, each of whom exaggerates (often to the point of eccentricity) one or another of these stable traits of the majority. Standing against the backdrop of the omnipresent sea, these uniques compensate with surface piquancy what they lack in spiritual vigor. Although still a novice, Miss Jewett conceives a group of credible, unselfconscious individuals. This book owes its richness to their presence.

Outstanding among the beached seamen are Captain Lant, who signs himself "condemned as unseaworthy," and Captain Sands, who is valued for being peculiar and somewhat visionary. They are interminable storytellers, gossiping and reminiscing about genealogy, town history, telepathy, and their marvelous adventures at sea. The latter's "Yankee shrewdness" in circumventing the Embargo and in stealing from cargo are patently unethical. Surprisingly, neither the basically honest captain nor the academically moral girls seem disturbed about his infractions.

Three other men make indelible impressions. The butcher who simply shuts up shop without a word and goes deep-sea fishing for two days affirms native independence. Craper, the red-haired, pale-faced consumptive who takes his children to the circus come hell or high water, is a paragon of indomitability. Danny, the lame, shy fisherman who always wears a red flannel shirt, is normally uncommunicative, and particularly so with the opposite sex. He permits himself one long parley with the girls in which he divulges more than he intends. Thereafter he is pleasant but silent, and flees mortified from a final farewell.

As may be expected, Miss Jewett is even more effective with the females. Spinsters and widows are in greatest frequence, and there are two pairs of elderly sisters. Mrs. Kew and Mrs. Bonny differ distinctly while sharing the role of self-reliant rural women. Mrs. Kew is unassuming, observes the formalities, reads books, and keeps her husband and the Deephaven Lighthouse going. Mrs. Bonny wears a man's coat and boots; comes to town on a black horse to sell butter, berries, and eggs; keeps house laxly; and is devastatingly straightforward in her opinions.

Mrs. Jim Patton and Miss Chauncey are the most memorable of the women. The Widow Jim is quick as a pickerel and twitters like a sparrow. She is privy to everyone's secrets, knows how to brew every variety of herb-tea, is commander-in-chief at funerals, and has all town pedigrees at tongue tip. (In many ways she is the prototype of Almira Todd in *The Country of the Pointed Firs*.) She becomes as friendly with the girls as she was helpful to Miss Brandon, but she keeps from them the story of the wound on her forehead. Miss Chauncey signifies an age that has passed. She dresses in rusty black satin gown and huge black bonnet, and she insists upon inhabiting the broken-down house that was once an elegant manor. It is indicative of her generation's inability to cope with the present that Miss Chauncey's mind fails many years before she dies.

The trend of Deephaven's deterioration may of course be read in the respective conditions of the Brandon and Chauncey houses. The chapter "Cunner-Fishing," however, provides a natural metaphor that scores the point more succinctly. Inside the hull of an old schooner which is going to pieces, the girls see a big flounder, one of whose fins is half gone. The flounder cannot get out, for the hole in the side of the schooner is not very wide and it is higher up than flounders ever swim. "Flounders always look so lazy, and as if they thought a great deal of themselves," says Helen. Like the rightly named flounder— partially disabled, lethargic, and self-satisfied—Deephaven is trapped in a world from which no escape seems possible.

As much as she venerates the past, Miss Jewett does not camouflage the obvious or inevitable. The Misses Brandons and Chaunceys were unfortunately dead or dying and no new generation of that "class of country people who preserve the best traditions of culture and of manners, from some divine inborn instinct"[6] is springing up to take their places. Some few representatives of the old families live on, but they are "like the conies of Scripture, a feeble folk." But the past has left an ineradicable stamp on Deephaven. With its Britannic faces and Chaucerian speech, it is more like an English than an American seacoast town. The sandbar which is slowly sealing the harbor mouth will effectively cut off communication with change.

The accompanying theme of country–city contrast is struck in the Preface. It is then embodied in the two urban girls on a rural vacation, who carry it through to the last chapter in their utterances and attitudes. To ensure a balanced perspective, Miss Jewett has them resent the canard that Deephaven is "a stupid, common country town." And the town heartily approves the complete absence of any manufacturing element.

The true unity of *Deephaven* abides in its pervasive atmosphere of beauty and serenity, in its tone of personal dignity and quiet humor. Miss Jewett's descriptions of the sea—particularly the scene from the lighthouse—and its significance to the natives catch and hold in a shimmering net the multicolored relationship of man and environment. The quaint expressions, the agelessly childlike folklore and superstitions of the region please and reassure.

To avert the impression that *Deephaven* is a blandish eclogue, and to refute Pattee's absurd statement that Miss Jewett "recorded only the things lovely and of good report,"[7] one may turn to the chapter "In Shadow," which pictures unsparingly the dismal life and death of a penniless family on a lonely cove. There are also the emaciated outskirts of Deephaven; the distressing squalor of the circus; the shabby, hopeless careers of the Kentucky Giantess and the pitiable lecturer; and the ugly implication of Mrs. Patton's drunken husband and the stone bottle. On the whole, *Deephaven* projects a segment of life ordinarily visible to the summer sojourner rather than the psychotic aberrations of a Winesburg or the covert flagrancies of a Peyton Place.

II *A Country Doctor*

A Country Doctor (1884), her second novel, appeared seven years and five books later. Though conforming with the requirements of a plot, a love affair, and a problem, it may better be classified in the Jewett canon as imaginative autobiography. In it Miss Jewett externalizes a common juvenile transfer-fantasy by replacing her actual parents with a pair of exotic, ill-starred mates, but she comfortably retains her real father and mother in the persons of Dr. Leslie and Mrs. Graham. Although Quinn places this above Howells' *Dr. Breen's Practice* and Ward's *Dr. Zay* as a study of the woman physician, Miss Jewett had no illusions about its rating as a novel. She could only recommend its "many excellent ideas, for which I must thank not only my father's teaching, but my father himself."[8] Life with father had taught her that "the village doctor comes nearer than anyone else to the true springs of village life, nearer even than the pastor."[9] *A Country Doctor* is her testimonial to that belief.

Nan Prince is a remarkable double for Sarah Orne Jewett; the only difference is her aim to become a doctor instead of a writer. A waif of nature, she prefers playing in woods and pastures to attending school. She accompanies the doctor on his visits, and rides a horse through the countryside when older. She is a daydreaming inventor of stories. Gradually her school lessons gain in attractiveness. She develops the provincial virtues of self-reliance, self-respect, and dignity. Restless and dissatisfied about household duties, she concludes that she is not the marrying sort. She grows into "a citizen of the world" for a time but eagerly returns to the home of her childhood.

The central conflict of her heart and mind is the nagging question of whether to marry or to follow a career. A number of social and personal factors complicate her decision. The double standard conspires with men in choosing a learned profession while forbidding women to do the same; and this situation Miss Jewett attacks with feministic relish. Unable to endorse medicine as a vocation for women in general, Nan avers that it is at least the proper study for her. Nan's relentless individualism sets up other hurdles; for in considering the welfare of the individual against the welfare of the group, she decides that preservation of the race is no longer the only objective. Some women are appointed by nature for other obligations than marriage. She cannot, in any case, marry the whole of herself; too great a share of her life would have to be submerged. To top all, she can like a man, but she hates "love."

Nan is also driven by the Puritan compulsion to be useful, one quickened by Dr. Leslie's appeal: "I want you to be a good woman, and I want you to be all the use you can." This statement she converts into a moral code and a mystic ordination. She does not attempt to pierce the enigma of her fate; she simply assumes a mood of passive receptivity for the "unmistakable command." As she matures, it becomes evident that a wise purpose has been at work with her and for her, quite outside her preferences. Her inclinations mingle with this greater force (eventually identified as God) to extract the best possible use of her gifts. In the end she rejects the supplications of her aunt (convention) and George Gerry (love) to fulfill her responsibility to herself in her God-plotted course.

Several familiar Jewett theses find incidental haven in the coils of this Victorian predicament. The country–city contrast appears in the diverse qualities of Oldfields and Dunport and in the rapid debasement of Nan's mother after she goes to Lowell. The superior value of rooted traditions is upheld through frequent comments about the flimsiness of modern houses, the increase in competitive spirit, the disappearance of "ideal" ladies and gentlemen, the worthlessness of sperm oil for lamps (symbolic of the past's fading light), Nan's penchant for retreating to her grandmother's farm when she is lonely or confused, and her final decision to settle in Oldfields, whose allegorical name verifies both its antiquarian associations and its rural locale.

Miss Jewett's theory of cumulative heredity exerts forceful influence upon Nan's ultimate resolve. By Miss Jewett's reckoning, inherited traits amass through several generations "until a child appears who is the heir of all the family wit and attractiveness and common sense, just as one person may inherit the worldly wealth of his ancestry." She believes that up to seven or eight years, children are "bundles of inheritances," later modified by individual assertion. So it becomes a convenience to attribute Nan's early waywardness to her infirm parents and her subsequent development to dormant qualities of earlier forebears.

The narrative progresses along chronological, biographical lines, with occasional steps backward taken by reminiscing characters. The opening scene is Dickensian Gothic, as are a number of suspenseful chapter endings. The narrator stands modestly on the perimeter of action but shows a deplorable tendency to lapse into direct preachment. She reports what people say, their way of saying, and their relations with others, and lets the story follow its own deliberate route. But the exigencies of continuous movement and "purpose" preclude the effects of solidity and leisure Miss Jewett usually creates.

The fundamental correspondence of character and environment is adduced through brief, unadorned imagery. For example, the funeral of Nan's mother occurs "with all nature looking on." These countryfolk who live closer to life, and therefore closer to death, hold a special key to the mysteries of existence. They come to "pay homage to Death rather than to the dead" in an occult communion unavailable to dwellers of cities.

A Country Doctor is as close to a problem novel as Miss Jewett ever comes. Part of its ineffectuality stems from a surplus of ideas, part in her handling them as a lecturer or minister might. The plot is hardly to be called complicated, but it was apparently more than she could manage without strain. Some half dozen characters—old Mrs. Thacher, Mrs. Graham, Mrs. Meeker, and the Jake and Martin Dyers—carry on with a vitality of their own; the rest are adapted to the service of the story. The love affair between Nan and George proves once and for all Miss Jewett's incapacity to reveal the urgencies of passion in youth. George is a two-dimensional cardboard figure who cannot impress upon Nan "that he was a man and she a girl." It is no wonder she votes for medicine instead of marriage. Miss Jewett's maidenly bias undercut the issue before it could be fought on its own merits.

III *A Marsh Island*

Miss Jewett's third novel, *A Marsh Island* (1885), which appeared one year after *A Country Doctor,* is also flawed by lack of psychological motivation and by insufficiency of plot. The triangle of young lovers sparks only the most perfunctory of conflicts. Customarily dramatic incidents—the lovers' quarrels— occur without especial tremor. The necessary accident to Dick Dale comes as an anomaly in the rhythmical unfolding of this bland narrative. But what fascinates Miss Jewett is not *what* happens but *where* it happens and, to a lesser degree, the persons to *whom* it happens. She opens an album of nature to a series of exquisite watercolors, with here and there a dab of human phenomena.

If it were not known that Miss Jewett modeled her locale on a real place with the disparate name of Hog Island, one would incline to deny the possibility of such an Elysium on earth. Marsh Island is selectively beautiful and untypical, with no signs of the blight that touches almost all Jewett territory. She paints with an artist's sensitivity to depths and angles, passing on with remarkable empathy the particular esthetic vision of Dick Dale. Newly arrived from the city, he abandons himself to the contours of landscape (the orchards, the water, the islets, the hills, flowers, the farmhouse) and to the interior shadings and textures (the delicate shapes, the patterns and relations of objects indoors). The purity of light that suffuses these scenes recalls unavoidably the Dutch masters Ruysdael and Vermeer.

Man in this great spaciousness of nature is unnaturally serene, with earthy assurance that whatever the outcome of his life, it will be in his favor. Like Millet's immutable peasants, the people of Marsh Island blend into the soil and derive from it the strength and wisdom of eternal evolution. Dan Lester receives a premonition from the wild rose as the hay-boat glides under it. The intimations of the "famous day for crows" are identical with those of Emerson's "The Humble-Bee." Even Dick Dale comes to realize that the difference between Doris Owen and a willow tree is one of degree.

Miss Jewett imparts a sense of epic to the lives of these farm folk diligently at work or play during the lusty days that precede the endless, encaging winter. Harvesting and disposing the salt hay of the marshes is the vivifying function, the symbolic communal heart of the farm. As summer wanes into autumn, apple-gathering and cider-making take up the cyclical pulse. The haymaking, the workers at supper, the Sunday evening social, the seasonal sunning of lard pots and stone jars have about them a primal air of rightness and durability.

Restraint and a too tender charm keep this novel from achieving the tragic proportions of Rölvaag's *Giants in the Earth*. Miss Jewett's view of character is determinedly external, a tentative omniscience which evades final responsibility. A spirit of gentle humor, which infiltrates thought and action, disarms virility and criticism. Pathos flows from the calculated invocation of the faded flag on young Israel Owen's grave and from the reiterated bestowal of human sensibility upon vegetation. Once again Miss Jewett confronts the materials for a profound and moving experience, but she has not the heart to stir them turbulently. To the end, *A Marsh Island* remains an idyll in the pastoral tradition —even to the stylized wooing.

Three contentious motifs furnish impetus and ornament to the action, and the foremost of these is Miss Jewett's perennial country–city contrast. The Owen family, ensconced in rustic felicity, becomes inadvertent host for a summer to Dick Dale, the thoroughly urban artist. Through a succession of varied devices, the country is shown to be virtuous, substantial, ageless, and optimistic; the city, dandified, doubtful, rootless, and negative. Persons, scenes, and activities of both ways of life are juxtaposed in a convincing victory for the marsh islanders. The sides are deployed as definitely as a football formation. The country contingent includes the Owen family (excepting the shallow mother), stolid Dan Lester, ingenious Tempy Kipp, and jolly Jim Fales; the city has indecisive Dick Dale, imperious Mrs. Winchester, flippant Bradish, and practical Mrs. Farley. Doris Owen, inheritress of the soil, is the backbone of descent, sure to breed the kind of children who will perpetuate the tribe. Old Israel Owen "with his flocks and herds and his love for his lands" is the farthest remove from "the mode of existence Dale had known best." Most effective in bringing out the disparity, however, are the antithetical Sunday evening social at the Owens' and the effete affair at Mrs. Winchester's. The arrival of Mrs. Winchester and Mrs. Farley at the Owen farmhouse serves the same purpose in slighter degree.

Love in altercation is a lesser theme not because it occupies the protagonists less but because Miss Jewett treats it with fantastic placidity. No passion erupts in open strife or in moments of private anguish during these misadventures of young love. The major notes are propriety, not poignancy; disappointment, not disaster. Dan sulks and stays away, Doris ingenuously wonders why, and Dick is neither here nor there. At the close, the country lovers come together as resistlessly as magnet and iron filing. Aside from some carefully modulated histrionics, neither displays undue perturbation. It must have been clear to everyone that love's uneven course must have to end inevitably in reconciliation.

The fate motif resounds in Dick Dale as it does in Nan Prince. Dick believes that "there are all sorts of powers and forces doing what they please with us," so he awaits the coming of "orders" in a comparable state of immobility. Miss Jewett, who muses solemnly on the mysteries of love and death, personally avows that neither is knowable this side of heaven. Both are manipulated by "strange powers" that make us "strangers even to ourselves." Love in the flesh was inconceivable to her.

Characters are created largely through the author's Olympian remarks, although the rustics comport themselves with distinguishable individuality. In assigning grass-roots virtues to the farmer instead of his wife, Miss Jewett makes a curious reversal. Israel Owen, the salt of the earth, is resourceful, understanding, and completely in harmony with his environment. Mrs. Owen is pretentious, self-delusive, selfish, and basically dissatisfied with her excellent lot. Doris Owen, who sometimes appears phlegmatic or anemic, is really meant to exhibit the serenity of a mature earth-goddess, certain that she can play hob with Dan's feelings and come off unscathed. An aura of dignity and secret knowledge always surrounds her. Dick Dale, sensitive but essentially without purpose, endorses the sterling merits of country life before he leaves by swearing that if he ever amounts to anything he will "thank those sincere, simple people for setting me the example." An honest, hard-working, moody man, Dan is a native son who will stay on the farm and make good. Two antipodal clowns fill out the sheaf: Jim Fales, a Shakespearean yokel who lends rural genius to several crucial scenes, particularly the one in which he probes Dick from the symbolic vantage of an apple tree; and Bradish, a phantom personality through most of the book, whose shiftless penury and lighthearted acceptance of *la vie bohème* crash discordantly against the solid granite walls of Israel Owen and Dan Lester when he finally materializes.

Arthur Hobson Quinn incisively indicates the significance of *A Marsh Island* when he says it is "a prose poem of earth and water, but it is not a great novel."[10]

IV *The Country of the Pointed Firs*

The Country of the Pointed Firs (1896), Miss Jewett's acknowledged masterpiece, is the result of twenty years of continual reconsideration of materials and refinement of methods. The long apprenticeship of essays and short stories on native scenes and themes reaches its culmination in this "best piece of regional fiction to have come out of nineteenth century America."[11] In the year between *The Second Jungle Book* and *Captains Courageous* Rudyard Kipling wrote Miss Jewett "to convey some small instalment of our satisfaction in that perfect little tale. It's immense —it is the very life. . . . I don't believe even you know how good that work is."[12] Praise from so athletic a personality at the vertex of his own career was praise indeed. Forsaking the formality of a traceable narrative line, Miss Jewett in *The Country of the Pointed Firs* returns to the irregularities of *Deephaven* but with a depth and tone impossible for her in 1877. Between that year and 1896 she had lost none of her informing sympathy; percipience and control had dilated immeasurably; maturity had set in. Thus, when she went over virtually the same ground, she could this time produce what Granville Hicks adjudges "the finest American achievement in its genre and a work of which we can be permanently proud."[13]

The most obvious qualitative advance is in the character of the narrator, who comes from the city to spend a summer in Dunnet Landing. The difference between her and the girlish narrators of *Deephaven* is really that between Sarah Orne Jewett at twenty-four and at forty-five. Quite out of the magazine-flinging age, Miss Jewett is not simply searching for novelty or titillation; and she is no longer a novice in human exchanges and feelings. Her narrator therefore urges natives into talk about themselves and the country but not in the impudent, conspiratorial manner of Helen Denis and Kate Lancaster. She injects sober, strategic questions without pressing the speaker if he shows any disinclination to proceed. She is not interested in talk for its own sake. She finds Captain Littlepage's reminiscences a trifle dull, and she intrudes a gentle note of reason when he seems to venture beyond probability. With fine compromise between self-consciousness and detachment, she transfers to the reader the incidents which make up the story. Mostly they come straight from the persons involved. When the narrator needs to enter, she does so with the air of an unobtrusive stage manager. Even her few summaries and commentaries are couched in a remote and uninsistent tone.

The narrator makes no pretense of becoming part and parcel of the community. She raises the curtain on the scene, lets the characters enact their roles, then lowers the curtain and silently steals away. Neither is she militantly the city woman. She falls "in love at first sight" with village and villagers, but is here and there reminded of the invisible screen between them. For example, Mrs. Todd remarks diagonally on her lack of provincial judgment and experience. The narrator assesses her failure to join the walking funeral as a sign that she does not really belong to Dunnet Landing. Little 'Johnny Bowden stares at her "with contemptuous surprise" when she displays ignorance about a common local fact of life. And, outlandishly, she wonders why wonderful Mrs. Blackett should have been wasted "on this lonely island of the northern coast."

Although the narrator never shakes off the odd sensation of being a "hermit crab in a cold new shell," she comes "near to feeling like a true Bowden" before she leaves. This carefully preserved dichotomy of separateness and empathy guarantees equable insight into the soul of this most typical Jewett domain. The narrator does not merely perform a necessary chore; she emerges with a strong integrity of her own.

Like Deephaven, Dunnet Landing is a composite which does not exist in all its aspects in any single spot. Miss Jewett goes as far as situating it "somewhere 'along shore' between the region of Tenants Harbor and Boothbay" but parries any attempts to pinpoint it. "It is not any real 'landing' or real 'harbor,'"[14] but the reality of Miss Jewett's whole experience and sensibility invests every detail of the place. Dunnet is an isolated maritime village chiefly approached by sea. Indeed, the sea is the veriest heart of its corporeal and spiritual subsistence. The land is not enough to live upon, and no house without a fishing boat can be sure of its daily comforts.

An even deeper feeling of dependence rises out of the sea— the eternal life-giving element. With the duple point of view she employed briefly in "A White Heron," "The Gray Man," "The Landscape Chamber," "The White Rose Road," and other stories, Miss Jewett encompasses the comprehensive vista that surrounds and determines the lives of her people. She takes a central stance from which she can see both land and sea—"the great army of the pointed firs, darkly cloaked and standing as if they waited to embark"—seeming to celebrate the solidity of roots in the ground, yet cherishing a route of escape. Whenever she wishes to savor the essence of interplay between human and natural forces she assumes this perspective—from the Landing, from the schoolhouse she uses as a writing sanctuary, from a hill on Green Island, or from the road on the way to the Bowden reunion. Over all she casts the revelatory luminescence of a Georges de la Tour or a Vlaminck.

Prosperity and progress have left Dunnet, and the village, once brisk, is now moribund. Events are of the kind considered commonplace in the cities, but their effects on the natives are as meaningful as the grand tragedies to the Greeks. Family feuds are enjoyed and perpetuated not for the sincerity of hatred but for something to talk and think about. Primitivism survives in numerous legends about indigenous specters and cannibals. The calendar is kept by the year one's oldest boy was born, or the winter a house burned down.

As in *Deephaven,* the facet remaining longest in the memory is the population. Again it is predominantly old, predominantly female. Everyone is gentle and helpful to each other and affectionate with discerning strangers. Beneath their Grant Wood exteriors are banked fires of almost volcanic light and heat. Such inward force is not wasted on petty excitements; it glows for friendship and kinship "as if from the inexhaustible burning heart of the earth." Through this continuing association with nature, Miss Jewett fixes the place of these people in the stream of immortality. Further elevation of native character comes through repeated identification with figures of classic history and myth: Almira Todd might belong to any age "like an idyl of Theocritus," and at different times she resembles a huge sibyl, a caryatid, Medea, Antigone. The narrator is like a messenger of Fate, Mrs. Hight has the features of a warlike Roman emperor, Esther might be Atalanta, and William is Jason. These are not local-color stereotypes parading for the entertainment of a sophisticated audience. They walk with dignity, speak with medieval resonance, and have regal connections with time.

Miss Jewett's beloved "ancient mariners" are the usual large old men who seem to dwell along the stony beaches and in the shoreline sheds, watching boats go out, cleaning fish, and tending lobster traps. They live in silent alliance with the sea, meditating upon the cogency of nature rather than any feeble contrivances of man. Chief of these is Captain Littlepage, a bookishly formal shipmaster "wrecked on the lee shore of age." He long ago retreated into memories, and now into fantasy. With his unshakeable conviction about an Arctic limbo which holds the secret of death and resurrection, he represents the last stage of the sad captains—lost to this life, not yet entered into the next. The narrator last sees him sitting behind a closed window, waiting for someone who never comes; symptomatically he is a captive behind the closed window of his addled mind, waiting for a day which will never return.

Two other men who would be regarded as eccentrics in a larger, less coherent community are Elijah Tilley and William Blackett. Elijah has no resources left from the vigorous life except the memory of his dead wife and the routines which remind him of her. He knits, keeps shipshape house, and constantly refers to his "poor dear." He barely avoids the completer compulsion of Dan'el Gunn, the tendency toward sex transition in the men and women of this devitalized area. Resembling his mother in build and shy of the ladies, William is "son an' daughter both." Significantly, he lacks his "mother's snap an' power o' seein' things just as they be." In other respects he avouches his birthright—simple, grave, gentle, self-reliant, and wise in the ways of nature.

The women of Dunnet Landing fare better. Whereas only two males (Captain Bowden and his son Johnny) cleave to normality, only two of the females are observably abnormal. Joanna Todd, as sadly mad as the King of Folly Island, is jilted through no fault of her own. She cuts herself off from all human contact on an uninhabited island, a penance conceived with masochistic fervor and maintained until death. Her behavior is a solemn parody of the whole region's relinquishment of life. With the creation of this character Miss Jewett demonstrates the control she acquired over the years. Joanna is not a ranting, disheveled Ophelia; she dresses and talks with consistent decorum. (Similarly, Miss Jewett eschews the sensationalism of the narrator's and Elijah's earlier counterparts.) The other abnormal woman, Abby Martin, is persuaded by several coincidences that she is the twin of Queen Victoria. Her otherwise arid life is enriched by this innocent delusion, underscoring the eternal question—how much of dream is reality? With characteristic acuity Almira declares upon leaving the old woman's house, "It ain't as if we left her all alone!"

The rest of the women represent three generations of self-sufficient, kindly sovereigns of the tribe. Mrs. Blackett stands for the lingering past, Mrs. Fosdick for the dignified and respectful present, and Esther Hight for the delayed heritage of the future. Supreme among these—and, in fact, all Jewett women—is Almira Todd; she is *genius loci* personified. It becomes quickly manifest that she is more than a lonely rural widow with just enough means to get along, for she has infinite inner reserves and seems to know everything. Her curiosity and inexhaustible industry have given her command over a wide range of practical matters from the distillation of arcane herb remedies to the steering of a dory. Generous, gregarious, good-humored, and garrulous, she can also be gruff and critical, acidulous in her dislikes, and expert at squelching malicious gossips. She is touchingly sentimental but evades open show of emotion by joking, retreating, or banging kitchen utensils. She has long been the director of her own destiny, and asserts her "governing mind" with finality. The universality of this physically and spiritually massive character rises out of her inherent involvement with nature and the tragedy of her love, which binds her in grief to Sophocles' Antigone. Sage as an oracle and limitlessly understanding, Almira dwarfs the narrator's sincerest tribute: "She was a great soul, was Mrs. Todd."

The action of *The Country of the Pointed Firs* is almost identical with that of *Deephaven*. Instead of two unfledged girls, one mature woman comes to an isolated coastal village, spends a summer observing and mixing with the natives, then returns to the city in the fall. There is no impelling plot with conflict, climax, and dénouement. Incident is sparse and passive, and this lack has betrayed many commentators into dismissing the structure as merely episodic, as a series of cameos, as anecdotes sewn together by a thin thread, as a scaffolding of narrative, or as charmingly subdued vignettes. Although the practice was to point vaguely to the unity of tone and setting, Matthiessen and Quinn have suggested that a deeper unity exists. More recently, Warner Berthoff and Hyatt H. Waggoner have analyzed this aspect of the book with ampler results.

Several unifying factors are continuously at work in this para-novel and an over-all pattern, though imprecise, is discernible. A speculative kind of unity is furnished by the peripatetic presence of the narrator who reports and correlates her encounters along shore, on the islands, and upcountry. A firmer integration emerges from the establishment of two symbolic focal points, the school-house and the Bowden Place. The first becomes for the narrator a hub of vision to the surrounding world, for she goes to it for a substantive interview or from it for new perspectives on the country and people. A properly bookish haven from rural attitudes, it is periodically necessary to her if she is to avert inundation by Almira Todd and her powerful contemporaries and customs. The narrator thus remains outseeing and self-examining, an instrument capable of appreciation yet of exercising her own critical values. Gradually the schoolhouse takes on importance not unlike that of the scaffold in *The Scarlet Letter*. The Bowden focal point recurs less frequently but with comparable potency. Underpinning the physical eminence of house and farm which

consolidates the outstretched community are the psychic attach-
ments which lend cohesion, hierarchy, and history to the image
of clan.

A third tissue of unity grows out of the spaced ceremonials of
funeral, visits, tribal reunion, and wedding, all of which impart
a sense of profound and ageless homogeneity. In these instances
Miss Jewett ranges into traditionary symbol; she raises New
England rite to the level of classic ritual by equating the spare,
dark lives of her own time and place with those of the ancient,
honorable past. The qualities required for peaceful transmission
of a culture—taste, skill, love, and modality—are conspicuous
here; moreover, they are like strong hands shaping and eternaliz-
ing a way of life. They are most elaborately on display in the
Bowden family reunion, an epitome of the mystique of family
communion. With suggestive references to sacred altar fires,
Pilgrim's Progress, the dynasty of age, Greeks celebrating a
victory, and antiquarian French festivities, Miss Jewett endows
the convocation with immemorial validity. These individuals
band indomitably together in perennial procession against the
catastrophes of nature and of time. Their leave-takings are
murmurous with "next summer," when they will once again
collectively repudiate the constraints of oblivion.

The presiding pattern of life in Dunnet Landing reflects the
unabating influence of the sea. In a fairly regular series of wave
movements Miss Jewett conveys the rhythmical rise and fall of
communal existence. Five crests of gayety or exultation are represented in the narrator's arrival and acquisition of the schoolhouse,
Green Island, the Bowden reunion, Esther Hight's farm, William's
wedding. Three troughs of sadness or tragedy are the walking
funeral, Shell-heap Island, the narrator's departure. Four sliding
walls of pathos and humor between these extremes are the
Littlepage story, the ride upcountry, and the visits to Elijah Tilley
and the queen's twin. There is as much asymmetry here as there
is in the climb and drop of successive waves. The impression of
incessant slow motion in a repetitive scheme is the same.

Three familiar Jewett themes, refined through a quarter-
century of exploration and treatment, flow through *The Country
of the Pointed Firs* without overrunning their banks as they
perceptibly do in her earlier works. The first of these supports a
Thoreauvian affinity of man and nature which is demonstrated
by group homage, in analogies, and through the pathetic fallacy,

but is best exemplified in Almira Todd. She has come "to an understanding with the primal forces of nature"; indeed, she seems to be "some force of nature personified." Her herbal remedies for mankind might even prove therapeutic for adverse winds at sea. Out of such intimacy come dignity, solidity, and faith in a God who fashioned man and nature out of the same essential stuff.

Reverence for the past and relative contempt for the present are other motivating attitudes. Captain Littlepage is the most explicit spokesman for the grandeur of Dunnet's yesterday and its doldrums of today. He decries the terrible decline of shipping and the appearance of modern architecture, new-fangled bicycles, and the loss of individuality. Almira, who is no less a lover of the past, sounds the realistic countertheme without fully comprehending that she does: "Oh, he used to be a beautiful man!"

Miss Jewett subordinates and balances the country–city contrast with a ripened appreciation for the values of both. Differences are not primarily pointed up by the narrator, as in *Deephaven*, but by the denizens of Dunnet Landing. Mrs. Todd expresses the opinion that city persons are prone to run themselves to death, although she also admits gravely that "There's all sorts o' folks in the country, same's there is in the city." Miss Jewett is now beyond the black-and-white stage of comparison between the two ways of life. Mrs. Fosdick's remarks about Joanna Todd suggest that detachment and change might be beneficial to an ingrown society. It has become clear that unvarying association of old surroundings, old customs, and old people may ultimately overwhelm the advantages of a common stock of knowledge, experience, and tastes.

Like *A Marsh Island*, *The Country of the Pointed Firs* is a lyric of nature and an epic of man with no bravura notes. Miss Jewett's tone of mingled pathos and humor, delightfully mellowed, predominates. In exposition, in description, and in dialogue she achieves an impeccable coalescence of level, tonality, and cadence. So fluid is the expression that the reader is seldom actively aware of reading. This is the rarest triumph of style.

Miss Jewett presents an escapist paradise in many respects—a garden of Hesperides where the world-weary may find asylum from the press of competition and complexity. But she has kept sentimentality at a minimum and has offset the beautiful with the barren. Green Island has its opposite number in Shell-heap

Island, the Bowden reunion countervails the Littlepage dis-orientation, Almira Todd is near kin to Joanna Todd. To this quality of muted and poised realism *The Country of the Pointed Firs* owes its recognition as the most notable depiction of locales, conditions, characters, and ideals in nineteenth-century rural New England.

V *The Tory Lover*

The Tory Lover (1901), Miss Jewett's last full-length work and her worst, appeared on a tide of neo-romantic historical novels which rose with the success of *Lorna Doone* in 1869 and reached flood proportions in the 1890's. American readers, stim-ulated by the fracas with Spain, fell avidly upon *Quo Vadis, The Prisoner of Zenda, To Have and to Hold,* and *When Knighthood Was in Flower.* In this realm of derring-do Miss Jewett had no business, and she knew it. To editor Scudder she wrote: "I am now pretty sure that it would not be wise *poor me* to undertake such a piece of work . . . and I have a great reluctance before the thought of turning aside into a new road."[15] Despite her wari-ness, she permitted Charles Dudley Warner to give her "the final push toward writing" the book.

She rationalized about always keeping "some of the old Ber-wick flowers in bloom," but she never quite shook the feeling that "It is certainly a dangerous thing to try to write something entirely different after one has been for years and years making stories as short and round as possible."[16] Henry James, who told her after he had read *The Tory Lover* that he considered the historical novel a fatally cheap genre, alluded to her own defects with gentlemanly evasion and then pleaded: "Go back to the dear Country of the Pointed Firs, *come* back to the palpable present *intimate* that throbs responsive, and that wants, misses, needs you, God knows, and suffers woefully in your absence."[17] But she sustained her crippling accident in the next year, and she published nothing of consequence thereafter.

In *The Tory Lover* Miss Jewett tries hard to suit the public appetite for flamboyant intrigue. She bows to the demand for exciting cloak-and-dagger action and clearly demonstrates that she has no stomach for it. To stretch suspense and add dramatic spice, she overdoes the cliff-hanging and nick-of-time techniques. Nevertheless, the story is seldom anything but polite and pallid. The pageantry and the intoxication of history in its bright moments are simply absent. Larding the story with some exploits of John Paul Jones fails to lift it out of the nineteenth-century women's-magazine conception of masculine risk and violence. When faced with an ungovernable situation Miss Jewett skips the scene itself and offers a report of it. Intent upon magnified and precipitous action, she scants her best talent—the casual creation of character through small and understated domestic activities in a run-of-the-mill day.

Characters are skin-deep and transparent. They meet and talk with awkward formality, except in chapter XXVIII where Miss Jewett copes with a familiar feminine circumstance. The constituents of drama are frequently foregathered but never kindled. The actors perform choreographically rather than galvanically; Mary Hamilton and Roger Wallingford are handsome robots moved by causes rather than feelings. They are less real then Doris Owen and Dan Lester, who at least are in league with the good earth. Paul Jones is meant to be a man of two natures but in the long run is merely two-dimensional. Dickson is correctly melodramatic as the villain, and Madam Wallingford is correctly formidable as the chief dowager. Master Sullivan has possibilities which are obscured by a too-thick cloud of secrecy. His wife, the most appealing character in the book, is a shrewd, salty, and able Meg Merrilies. Characterization is subordinated to intensity of action, with rather disastrous consequences to both.

But Miss Jewett's evocative pictorial art does not desert her. Berwick during the Revolutionary era is scrupulously and lovingly portrayed, as are the traditions and distinctions which bind its aristocrats and commoners. The description of Mill Prison is alive and realistic. But too often Miss Jewett tries to achieve with language what she lacks in rapture or energy. Her ordinarily unself-conscious prose is pocked with romantic grandiloquence, sententious pomp, sentimental clichés, and spineless metaphors unnatural to her. And, after all the knots are unraveled, Miss Jewett evades the long-awaited clasp of the harried lovers. Passion and tragedy are not in her thesaurus.

In moments of fervor and tears Miss Jewett displays a remarkable—for her—dislocation of sympathy. She remains the detached spectator while her women suffer and coolly recounts their woes. The insight and the intimacy of the sketches and short stories are nowhere evident. The historical point of view lodges her so far from her people that she never comes to know them.

The fabric of *The Tory Lover* is woven out of the divided loyalties during the early days of the Revolution, and complications rising out of the misunderstanding and separation of young love. Two women (mother and lover) engage in basic struggle for possession of a man. To the detriment of the book, the theme of love-conflict evolves with less potency. Roger Wallingford's perplexity in regard to British or American allegiance is more vividly motivated than his distress over parting from Mary. The hard pull of nativity against ancestry apparently left little vigor in his heart for love's vicissitudes.

In her last book Miss Jewett returns to her earliest theme: the past holds the roots of value; the present is a falling of leaves. The economic and spiritual decline of New England which she deplores throughout her literary life is here caught at its beginnings. Berwick prosperity was largely due to trade with England; rebellion against the mother country has now cut off that outlet. "The busy, quick-enriching days of the past seemed to be gone forever, and poverty and uncertainty had replaced them." There were no comparable markets to turn to. Berwick would have to live hereafter on accumulated stocks and memories.

Heredity and fate vie with each other to control the direction of life. The Hamiltons are blessed with "some strain of good blood" which had brought them from meager childhood to a state of current luxury and would sustain them through future trials. Mary Hamilton, however, is "driven by the whip of Fate," which connotes a resistless, perhaps pagan, power ruling co-equally with God. But in one of Jones's late speeches Miss Jewett reclaims the orthodox, Christian mainspring: "I believe now that God's providence has brought me to your side," he sighs feelingly.

The Tory Lover is the imprudence of a thrush trying to roar like a lion.

CHAPTER 7

The Remainder and the Reputation

I *Children's Stories, Poetry*

IN COMMON with her contemporary sisters of the quill, Sarah
Orne Jewett produced numerous stories for children, some of
which she collected in *Play Days* (1878). For the slightly older
set she wrote *Betty Leicester* (1890) and *Betty Leicester's
Christmas* (1894, 1899). None is tinged with greatness; they are
important only as they exhibit one or another of the qualities
which mark her more mature work.

Immediately prominent is her flair for finger-wagging morali-
zation. Fondly but firmly, like the maiden aunt she was, she
advocates through illustrative episodes the standard virtues of
honesty, respect, industry, prudence, charity, self-reliance, decorum, and humility. She tells no rattling tales, nor does she
overstate. Pathos and humor predominate in these miniature
domestic comedies in which she presents a world of fantasy
where stuffed owls talk and pepper shakers spring to life.
Mimicry of adulthood enters when dolls are given medication,
and tea is served in an actual house built to juvenile scale.
Mostly it is a girl's world, just as Miss Jewett's adults inhabit a
woman's world; boys are incidental, never so sensitive or arti-
culate as girls, and usually clumsy. Little girls are incipient
mothers and housekeepers with rampant maternal instincts.

Most indicative of her subsequent style is the balance of realism
she achieves in the *Play Days* stories. With the meticulous care
she later expended on more significant material, she conveys
striking details of interior and exterior scenes. At least twice
she verges upon naturalism in her descriptions of the torn and
bloody woodchuck and the necklace of flies. On the social level,
she verifies children's capacity to be as squeamish and snobbish
as adults. She sought no special applause for these insights:

"When people sometimes remark upon the realistic personality of one of my book children I go back in thought to some moment of childish play and say, 'That did not take any work. It is just a child I knew once, lifted out of those days and feloniously transferred to my book. I ought to be arrested for kidnapping, because it was nothing else.' "[1]

Miss Jewett occasionally turned her hand to verse, some two-score examples of which found their way into print. In 1916 Mark A. De Wolfe Howe collected nineteen short pieces and guided them through the press at her family's request. *Verses* is not a distinguished volume. One may point to the poignant desolation in the second poem to her father and to the jubilant lyricism of "Top of the Hill." Beyond these two poems, there is little more than rhymed platitude. She extracts her topics from the moving stream of experience but treats them with equanimous superficiality. She avoids complexity in language and density in figures. Her meters are pedestrian. In an early letter to Scudder she expresses doubt about her poetizing; her intuition was true.

II *The Story of the Normans*

Between appearances of such sturdy short stories as "A White Heron" and "Miss Tempy's Watchers" Miss Jewett brought out *The Story of the Normans* (1887) in Putnam's series of national histories. She was sincere in wanting an authentic formulation and did what she considered adequate research. The result is a fragment of hack work which begins with Rolf, the first duke of the Normans, and peters out after William the Conqueror. Sarah Jewett had neither the training, the perspective, the profundity, nor the style necessary for such a book. It contains a pleasantly uncomplicated survey of early English life and times, in which she relieves herself of several amateur theories about race motivation and the bases of character.

Her expression lacks the strength and stamina for extended documentary presentation. Although her evidence is orderly and interesting, her language and tone have a dimity touch. She tries to domesticate and colloquialize history, and she is lured without effort from the strict path of history into colorful byways of legend and anecdote. She addresses the reader with chatty familiarity, re-creates purported conversations between historic personages, and interjects excited exclamations. Not infrequently she enters the thoughts of her protagonists to relay what is going on there. And she tends toward prettification, treating William the Conqueror's bastardy as a picturesque idyll.

She declares that history is more than "the story of this monarch or that," and she does deal in elements of home life, social customs, law, morality, and religion. But most of her attempts at analysis of ethos yield sooner or later to storytelling. It is instructive, however, to note the relation to her fiction and sketches of three guiding motifs in *The Story*. First, her conviction that climate profoundly affects the enterprise and intelligence of individuals and the mores of race. Second, her faith in heredity as a determining factor in character. She presumes for the Normans a superiority of mind and heart which stems from the Vikings and passes through the English to the Americans. So strong is this influence that she claims ability to separate Saxon from Norman in Berwick. Third, her feminist bias, which emerges in compassionate apostrophe—"poor women!"—and in disputable statement: "Both Saxons and Normans paid great deference to the instinctive opinions of women."

III *Growing Reputation*

Excluding the volumes discussed in this chapter, Sarah Orne Jewett's work is a considerable contribution to American literature. Of her novels, *Deephaven* and *The Country of the Pointed Firs* will always extend a vital personal record of the people, conditions, and values of nineteenth-century rural New England to generations desiring intimate knowledge of the national past. Varying estimates, in precise figures or sweeping phrases, have been offered as to the possibilities of survival of Miss Jewett's short stories, and anthologists have narrowed these down to particular preferences. My own feeling is that these will continue to be rated high among their kind on American lists: "A White Heron," "Marsh Rosemary," "The Dulham Ladies," "Miss Tempy's Watchers," "The Town Poor," "By the Morning Boat," "Miss Esther's Guest," "The Flight of Betsey Lane," "The Hiltons' Holiday," and "The Guests of Mrs. Timms." At least ten others are only a rung below. All of the collected sketches contain the pith of that special corner of Maine which, despite inherent variations, is known the world over.

It has been shown that Miss Jewett's finished art is deficient in some of the significant phases of a mature culture. She was neither philosopher nor sociologist, but she was an observer and interpreter who did the type of observing that precedes speculation and the kind of interpreting that resists collectivization. She has this in common with many American writers who have been more concerned with substance than with subtlety, and she fits, therefore, into a middle place in several lines of development in American literature. In style and content she relates to Washington Irving; in mystical advocacy of nature to the transcendentalists Emerson, Thoreau, and Whitman; in gentility of realism to Howells and Henry James; in choice of locale and characters to Harriet Beecher Stowe; in themes, if not treatment, to Hawthorne. Without ascribing definite influence, it may safely be said that her grace of expression has been perpetuated in similar fields by Willa Cather and John Steinbeck; that her characters have reappeared with appropriate mutations in the poetry of E. A. Robinson and Robert Frost; that her situations, if not moods, are to be found in Edith Wharton's New England aspect; and that her concept of a fruitful, renewable York-napatawpha county is not unlike Faulkner's mythos.

With just enough perspective and more than enough perspicacity, Willa Cather was the first to proclaim Sarah Orne Jewett a writer of unique importance. Singling out *The Country of the Pointed Firs*, Miss Cather dwelt upon the pleasures that new readers would discover upon reading this "masterpiece." Almost as famous as Miss Jewett's best book is Miss Cather's oft-repeated attestation: "If I were asked to name three American books which have the possibility of a long, long life, I would say at once, 'The Scarlet Letter,' 'Huckleberry Finn,' and 'The Country of the Pointed Firs.' I can think of no others that confront time and change so securely."[2]

Twenty years after Miss Jewett's death, Francis O. Matthiessen, her first biographer, was equally impressed with the prospect of her literary longevity. "She has withstood the onslaught of time, and is secure within her limits."[3] More recently, praise from critics and scholars of excellent repute has reaffirmed this early enthusiasm. To cite only three: Van Wyck Brooks, "No one since Hawthorne had pictured this New England world with such exquisite freshness of feeling";[4] Carlos Baker, ". . . the most distinguished career among all the writers of regional fiction. Sarah Orne Jewett developed her gifts more rapidly, maintained them at a higher level, and employed them with greater dexterity and control than did any of her predecessors in the field";[5] editors Leon Howard, Louis B. Wright, and Carl Bode, "It was Miss Jewett's *The Country of the Pointed Firs* which brought the local color novel to its highest degree of artistic perfection in nineteenth century America."[6]

It is not too much to claim that Sarah Orne Jewett is without peer among her contemporaries in the reliable depiction of her chosen time, place, and personalities.

Notes and References

Chapter One

1. *Country By-Ways*, p. 32. In "Looking Back on Girlhood," *Youth's Companion*, LXV (January 7, 1892), 6, Miss Jewett recalls: "My grandfather died in my eleventh year, and presently the Civil War began. From that time the simple village life was at an end."

2. Pp. 117-18.

3. *Letters of Sarah Orne Jewett*, ed. Annie Fields (Boston, 1911), p. 125.

4. Francis Otto Matthiessen, *Sarah Orne Jewett* (Boston, 1929), p. 38.

5. John Eldridge Frost, *Sarah Orne Jewett* (Kittery Point, Me., 1960), p. 72.

6. Fields, *Letters*, pp. 14-15. Writing to Sarah Wyman Whitman a dozen years later, Miss Jewett reveals even closer attachment to that "earlier and most incomparable" company: "I look upon that generation as the one to which I really belong,—I who was brought up with grand-fathers and grand-uncles and aunts for my best play-mates. They were not the wine that one can get at so much the dozen now!" *Ibid.*, p. 111.

7. *Sarah Orne Jewett Letters*, ed. Richard Cary (Waterville, Me., 1956), pp. 33-34.

8. Frances Perry Dudley, *The Mid-Century in Exeter* (Exeter, N. H., 1943), p. 16.

9. Jewett, "Looking Back on Girlhood," p. 6: "I have tried already to give some idea of my father's character in my story of 'The [sic] Country Doctor,' but all that is inadequate to the gifts and character of the man himself. He gave me my first and best knowledge of books by his own delight and dependence upon them, and ruled my early attempts at writing by the severity and simplicity of his own good taste."

10. LaSalle Corbell Pickett, *Across My Path: Memories of People I Have Known* (New York, 1916), p. 143.

11. All quotations between footnotes 10 and 11 are from Miss Jewett's "Looking Back on Girlhood."

12. Miss Jewett's statements about *The Pearl of Orr's Island* may be found in the 1893 Preface to *Deephaven*, pp. 3-4; in Fields, *Letters*, pp. 46-47; and in Cary, *Letters*, p. 65.

13. Cary, *Letters*, pp. 19-20; see also pp. 64-65; and Preface to *Deephaven* (1894).

14. Willa Cather, *Alexander's Bridge* (Boston, 1922), p. vii. Fourteen years later in *Not Under Forty* (New York, 1936), p. 88, Miss Cather recalled the last sentence as: "You must know the world before you can know the village."

15. *A History of American Literature Since 1870* (New York, 1915), pp. 220-21.

16. *Country By-Ways*, p. 116.

17. Cary, *Letters*, p. 27.

18. Henry James, "Mr. and Mrs. James T. Fields," *Atlantic Monthly*, CXVI (July 1915), 30.

Chapter Two

1. Vernon Louis Parrington, *Main Currents in American Thought* (New York, 1930), III, 63. He partially recants, however, on pages 65-66.

2. Fields, *Letters*, pp. 195-96.

3. Samuel T. Pickard, *Life and Letters of John Greenleaf Whittier* (Boston, 1895). II, 718.

4. Fields, *Letters*, p. 82.

5. *Deephaven*, p. 245.

6. Mrs. Kew is in *Deephaven;* Hannah West, "A Bit of Shore Life"; Nan Prince, *A Country Doctor;* Polly Finch, "Farmer Finch"; Ann Floyd, "Marsh Rosemary"; Eliza Peck, "Miss Peck's Promotion"; Esther Jaffrey, "A Village Shop"; Mercy Bascom, "Fair Day"; Hannah Pinkham, "The Quest of Mr. Teaby"; Ann Ball, "The Taking of Captain Ball"; Betsey Lane, "The Flight of Betsey Lane"; Maria Durrant, "A Second Spring"; Mrs. Peter Lunn, "All My Sad Captains"; Almira Todd, Mrs. Blackett, and Esther Hight, *The Country of the Pointed Firs;* Cynthy Dallett, "Aunt Cynthy Dallett"; Mrs. Sullivan, *The Tory Lover.*

7. Pickett, p. 145.

8. "The Art of Miss Jewett," *Atlantic Monthly*, XCIV (October 1904), 497.

Chapter Three

1. M. A. De Wolfe Howe, "Sarah Orne Jewett," *Atlantic Monthly*, CIV (August 1909), 281.

2. Cary, *Letters*, p. 28.

3. Mildred Howells (ed.), *Life in Letters of William Dean Howells* (New York, 1928), II, 15.

4. Fields, *Letters*, p. 123.

5. Quoted by Willa Cather in her Preface to *The Best Stories of Sarah Orne Jewett* (Boston, 1925), I, ix.

6. Fields, *Letters*, p. 165.
7. Matthiessen, p. 90.
8. Fields, *Letters*, p. 114.
9. Cary, *Letters*, p. 90.
10. Pickett, pp. 146-47.
11. Kitty Tennant appears in "Mr. Bruce"; Kate Lancaster, *Deephaven;* Bessie Thorne, "Miss Sydney's Flowers"; Mary Leslie, "Good Luck: A Girl's Story"; Dan'el Gunn, "An Autumn Holiday"; Elijah Tilley, *The Country of the Pointed Firs;* Danny, *Deephaven;* William Blackett, *The Country of the Pointed Firs;* Elisha, "By the Morning Boat"; Andrew Phillips, "Andrew's Fortune"; Daniel Lewis, "The Mate of the Daylight"; Parker Jenkins, "A Landless Farmer"; Johnny Harris, "The Night Before Thanksgiving"; the Honorable Joseph K. Laneway, "A Native of Winby"; Henry Stroud, "A New Parishioner."
12. Fields, *Letters*, pp. 118-19.
13. *Ibid.*, p. 196.
14. Cary, *Letters*, p. 29.
15. Fields, *Letters*, pp. 51-52.
16. Matthiessen, p. 103.
17. M. A. De Wolfe Howe, *Memories of a Hostess* (Boston, 1922), p. 300.
18. Fields, *Letters*, p. 196.
19. Frost, p. 144.
20. Cary, *Letters*, p. 28.
21. Fields, *Letters*, p. 81.
22. Matthiessen, pp. 89-90.

Chapter Four

1. Van Wyck Brooks, *New England: Indian Summer* (New York, 1940), p. 353.
2. Cary, *Letters*, p. 29.
3. *A History of American Literature Since 1870*, p. 235.
4. "In some ways it is one of the very best bits of writing I have ever done," Miss Jewett wrote Henry Mills Alden. "There is one point in its favour which I never thought of before: and that is, a sketch which has something to say about a girl's 'rough-riding' is a little of a novelty in magazine literature. This has at least the virtue of being true, of my horse, the 'farm' and the old parsonage—which is more than I can say for my sketches usually. Isn't it a curious thing that most people who read the two would probably call this made-up, and the one which you already have ["An Autumn Holiday"], drawn from life?" Cary, *Letters*, p. 36.
5. *The Best Stories of Sarah Orne Jewett*, I, xiv.

Chapter Five

1. In their headpiece to four Jewett stories in *American Local-Color Stories* (New York, 1941), Harry R. Warfel and G. Harrison Orians nominate "no fewer than thirty-two" as "memorable."
2. Fields, *Letters*, p. 81.
3. "The Art of Jewett's *Pointed Firs*," *New England Quarterly*, XXXII (March 1959), 35.
4. *The Best Stories of Sarah Orne Jewett*, I, xvi.
5. "The Gray Man," in *A White Heron and Other Stories*.
6. For her comments on "Lady Ferry," see Fields, *Letters*, p. 226; on "The Gray Man," *ibid.*, pp. 19-20, 39.
7. *Ibid.*, p. 60.
8. *Friday Nights*, p. 192.
9. *Sarah Orne Jewett*, p. 147.
10. In *Acres of Flint* (Washington, D.C., 1951), p .110, Perry D. Westbrook, who finds Betsey's flight implausible from the standpoint of psychological reality, maintains that capability of decisive action, like muscle, atrophies from disuse. This may be true in general, but he appears to underestimate the toughness of fibre in nineteenth-century, rural New England women.
11. Matthiessen, p. 97.
12. Fields, *Letters*, p. 186.

Chapter Six

1. Cary, *Letters*, p. 28.
2. "The Art of Miss Jewett," p. 495.
3. Pickard, II, 654.
4. Frost, p. 47.
5. *The Best Stories of Sarah Orne Jewett*, I, x.
6. *Deephaven* (1894), pp. 5-6.
7. *The Development of the American Short Story* (New York, 1923), p. 262.
8. Fields, *Letters*, p. 195.
9. Pickett, p. 145.
10. *American Fiction*, p. 326.
11. Carlos Baker, "Delineation of Life and Character," *Literary History of the United States*, ed. Robert E. Spiller *et al.* (New York, 1948), II, 845.
12. Fields, *Letters*, p. 9.
13. *The Great Tradition* (New York, 1933), p. 103.
14. Cary, *Letters*, p. 89.
15. *Ibid.*, p. 92.

16. *Ibid.*, p. 94.

17. Ferman Bishop, "Henry James Criticizes *The Tory Lover,*" *American Literature,* XXVII (May 1955), 264.

Chapter Seven

1. Pickett, pp. 144-45.
2. *The Best Stories of Sarah Orne Jewett,* I, xviii.
3. *Sarah Orne Jewett,* p. 145.
4. *New England: Indian Summer,* p. 353.
5. *Literary History of the United States,* II, 845.
6. *American Heritage* (Boston, 1955), II, 316.

Selected Bibliography

PRIMARY SOURCES

Deephaven. Boston: James R. Osgood & Co., 1877.

Play Days. Boston: Houghton, Osgood & Co., 1878. (Fifteen short stories for children.)

Old Friends and New. Boston: Houghton, Osgood & Co., 1879. (Contains: "A Lost Lover," "A Sorrowful Guest," "A Late Supper," "Mr. Bruce," "Miss Sydney's Flowers," "Lady Ferry," "A Bit of Shore Life.")

Country By-Ways. Boston: Houghton, Mifflin & Co., 1881. (Contains: "River Driftwood," "Andrew's Fortune," "An October Ride," "From a Mournful Villager," "An Autumn Holiday," "A Winter Drive," "Good Luck: A Girl's Story," "Miss Becky's Pilgrimage.")

The Mate of the Daylight, and Friends Ashore. Boston: Houghton, Mifflin & Co., 1884. (Contains: "The Mate of the Daylight," "A Landless Farmer," "A New Parishioner," "An Only Son" "Miss Debby's Neighbors," "Tom's Husband," "The Confession of a House-Breaker," "A Little Traveler.")

A Country Doctor. Boston: Houghton, Mifflin & Co., 1884.

A Marsh Island. Boston: Houghton, Mifflin & Co., 1885.

A White Heron and Other Stories. Boston: Houghton, Mifflin & Co., 1886. (Contains: "A White Heron," "The Gray Man," "Farmer Finch," "Marsh Rosemary," "The Dulham Ladies," "A Business Man," "Mary and Martha," "The News from Petersham," "The Two Browns.")

The Story of the Normans. New York: G. P. Putnam's Sons, 1887.

The King of Folly Island and Other People. Boston: Houghton, Mifflin & Co., 1888. (Contains: "The King of Folly Island," "The Courting of Sister Wisby," "The Landscape Chamber," "Law Lane," "Miss Peck's Promotion," "Miss Tempy's Watchers," "A Village Shop," "Mère Pochette.")

Betty Leicester. Boston: Houghton, Mifflin & Co., 1890. (For older children.)

Tales of New England. Boston: Houghton, Mifflin & Co., 1890. (Contains: "Miss Tempy's Watchers," "The Dulham Ladies," "An Only Son," "Marsh Rosemary," "A White Heron," "Law Lane," "A Lost Lover," "The Courting of Sister Wisby.")

Strangers and Wayfarers. Boston: Houghton, Mifflin & Co., 1890. (Contains: "A Winter Courtship," "The Mistress of Sydenham Plantation," "The Town Poor," "The Quest of Mr. Teaby," "The

Luck of the Bogans," "Fair Day," "Going to Shrewsbury," "The
Taking of Captain Ball," "By the Morning Boat," "In Dark New
England Days," "The White Rose Road.")

A Native of Winby and Other Tales. Boston: Houghton, Mifflin & Co.,
1893. (Contains: "A Native of Winby," "Decoration Day," "Jim's
Little Woman," "The Failure of David Berry," "The Passing of
Sister Barsett," "Miss Esther's Guest," "The Flight of Betsey
Lane," "Between Mass and Vespers," "A Little Captive Maid.")

Betty Leicester's English Xmas. Baltimore: privately printed, 1894.
Published as *Betty Leicester's Christmas* by Houghton, Mifflin
& Co., 1899. (For older children.)

The Life of Nancy. Boston: Houghton, Mifflin & Co., 1895. (Contains:
"The Life of Nancy," "Fame's Little Day," "A War Debt," "The
Hiltons' Holiday," "The Only Rose," "A Second Spring," "Little
French Mary," "The Guests of Mrs. Timms," "A Neighbor's
Landmark," "All My Sad Captains.")

The Country of the Pointed Firs. Boston: Houghton, Mifflin & Co.,
1896.

The Queen's Twin and Other Stories. Boston: Houghton, Mifflin &
Co., 1899. (Contains: "The Queen's Twin," "A Dunnet Shep-
herdess," "Where's Nora?," "Bold Words at the Bridge," "Martha's
Lady," "The Coon Dog," "Aunt Cynthy Dallett," "The Night
Before Thanksgiving.")

The Tory Lover. Boston: Houghton, Mifflin & Co., 1901.

An Empty Purse. Boston: Merrymount Press, 1905. (One short story.)

Letters of Sarah Orne Jewett. Boston: Houghton, Mifflin & Co., 1911.
Edited by Annie Fields.

Verses. Boston: Merrymount Press, 1916.

Sarah Orne Jewett Letters. Waterville, Maine: Colby College Press,
1956. Edited by Richard Cary.

SECONDARY SOURCES

I. Genealogy

JEWETT, FREDERIC CLARKE. *History and Genealogy of the Jewetts in
America* (Rowley, Mass., 1908. 2 vols). Account of SOJ's immediate family; a two-page report on her is in Vol. II, pp. 647-50.

II. Biography

FROST, JOHN ELDRIDGE. *Sarah Orne Jewett* (Kittery Point, Maine,
1960). Almost entirely biographical; provides much data and
documentation missing in Matthiessen.

MATTHIESSEN, FRANCIS OTTO. *Sarah Orne Jewett* (Boston, 1929).
Appreciative essay on SOJ's life and works, but lacks specific
dates, details, and documentation.

III. Bibliography

WEBER, CLARA C. and CARL J. WEBER. *A Bibliography of the Published Writings of Sarah Orne Jewett* (Waterville, Maine, 1949). Descriptive check list rather than a definitive bibliography; useful for chronology of first appearances and secondary sources.)

IV. Biographical and Critical Materials
In books and brochures:

BISHOP, FERMAN. *The Sense of the Past in Sarah Orne Jewett*. University of Wichita Bulletin. University Studies No. 41. (Wichita Kansas, February 1959), 8 pp. SOJ's attachment to the past endowed her realistic literary method with imaginative color and density of perspective.

BROOKS, VAN WYCK. *New England: Indian Summer* (New York, 1940), pp. 347-53. Impressionistic biographical sketch suggesting debt to Howells and similarity to Hawthorne.

BUCHAN, ALEXANDER M. *"Our Dear Sarah"; An Essay on Sarah Orne Jewett*. Washington University Studies—New Series. Language and Literature—No. 24 (St. Louis, 1953), 39 pp. SOJ's subjective principles of literary creation are to the same purpose as Wordsworth's.

CATHER, WILLA (ed.). *The Best Stories of Sarah Orne Jewett* (Boston, 1925), I, ix-xix. Strongly favorable appraisal by SOJ's most successful disciple; rates *The Country of the Pointed Firs* with *The Scarlet Letter* and *Huckleberry Finn*.

————. *Not Under Forty* (New York, 1936), pp. 76-95. First part, a condensation of the Preface in *Best Stories* (see above) omitting the comparison; the rest, personal impressions of SOJ and commentary on her art.

GARNETT, EDWARD. *Friday Nights* (New York, 1922), pp. 189-98. Generally commendatory review of SOJ's work; underscores her gift of drawing from nature and fidelity to feminine imagination.

HARKINS, E. F. *Famous Authors (Women)* (Boston, 1901), pp. 43-58. Published in 1902 as *Little Pilgrimages Among the Women Who Have Written Famous Books* by Harkins and C. H. L. Johnston, same pagination. Broad survey of SOJ's life, work, and working methods.

HICKS, GRANVILLE. *The Great Tradition* (New York, 1933), pp. 101-5. Despite obvious limitations, SOJ had exceptional powers and perception which made her master of a tiny realm.

HOWE, M. A. DE WOLFE. *Memories of a Hostess* (Boston, 1922), pp. 281-305. Recollection of SOJ's travels and wide circle of genteel friends, particularly Annie Fields.

————. *Who Lived Here?* (Boston, 1952), pp. 88-100. Affable

biographical essay, with five photographs of the Jewett house in South Berwick and a commemorative poem to SOJ.

PARRINGTON, VERNON LOUIS. *Main Currents in American Thought* (New York, 1930), III, 63-66. Although SOJ reached for a more adequate realism, the roots of her art were too deep in Brahmin soil for her to turn naturalist.

PATTEE, FRED LEWIS. *A History of American Literature Since 1870* (New York, 1915), pp. 231-35. Likens SOJ slightly to Hawthorne, more to Mrs. Gaskell and the earlier Howells.

————. *The Development of the American Short Story* (New York, 1923), pp. 259-63. By rapid example and by suggestion, SOJ is shown to be unlike Poe, Twain, or Kipling; like Irving, Cable, and Austen.

PICKETT, LASALLE CORBELL. *Across My Path: Memories of People I Have Known* (New York, 1916), pp. 143-48. Includes SOJ's tribute to her father's wisdom in exposing her to the places and people later depicted in her writings.

QUINN, ARTHUR HOBSON. *American Fiction* (New York, 1936), pp. 324-30. Chronological account of SOJ's development as an artist, with concise reviews of her most important works.

RICHARDS, LAURA E. *Stepping Westward* (New York, 1931), pp. 361-70. Intimate glimpses of SOJ's surroundings and activities in Annie Fields's Boston home and in the Jewett house in South Berwick.

RICKER, JENNIE DE R. *South Berwick, Me.: Pages From the Past* [South Berwick, 1936], 17 pp. Useful historical data on SOJ's home town and its inhabitants.

SPOFFORD, HARRIET PRESCOTT. *A Little Book of Friends* (Boston, 1916), pp. 21-42. Characterization of SOJ out of personal relationship and excerpts from her letters.

WEST, REBECCA (ed.). *The Only Rose and Other Tales by Sarah Orne Jewett* (London, 1937), pp. 7-14. SOJ's universe is emasculated but she has every necessary literary quality and writes out of an abundant liberal culture.

WESTBROOK, PERRY D. *Acres of Flint* (Washington, D.C., 1951), pp. 45-81 *et passim*. Summaries, analyses, and comparisons of SOJ's work with that of Willa Cather, Helen Hunt Jackson, George Eliot and Alice Brown.

WINSLOW, HELEN M. *Little Journeys in Literature* (Boston, 1902), pp. 63-72. (Published also in 1903 as *Literary Boston of To-day*, same pagination.) Generalized biographical account based on personal interview and quotations from secondary sources.

In periodicals:

ALDEN, JOHN. "Sarah Orne Jewett to Mellen Chamberlain," *Boston Public Library Quarterly*, IX (April, 1957), 86-96. Ten letters—

August 5, 1874 to Febraury 2, 1899—and a humorous verse to this judge of the Boston Municipal Court who later became Librarian of Boston Public Library.

BENTZON, TH. "Le Roman de la Femme-Médecin," *Revue Des Deux Mondes*, LXVII (February 1, 1885), 598-632. Extended summary and critique of *A Country Doctor*.

BERTHOFF, WARNER. "The Art of Jewett's *Pointed Firs*," *New England Quarterly*, XXXII (March, 1959), 31-53. SOJ's art lies in suffusing a vanishing local pattern of community life with durable colors of legend and the solemnity of history.

BISHOP, FERMAN. "Henry James Criticizes *The Tory Lover*," *American Literature*, XXVII (May, 1955), 262-64. In a letter—October 5, 1901—James declares his lack of sympathy with experiments in the "historic" novel and advises SOJ to return to the country of the pointed firs.

————. "Sarah Orne Jewett's Ideas of Race," *New England Quarterly*, XXX (June, 1957), 243-49. SOJ's preparatory reading for *The Story of the Normans* led her to prefer the Norman heritage to that of the Saxon in English descent.

CARY, RICHARD. "Jewett, Tarkington, and the Maine Line," *Colby Library Quarterly*, IV (February, 1956), 89-95. Tarkington would have allayed SOJ's "dark fear" of "the tourist or summer citizen," as expressed in the 1893 Preface to *Deephaven*.

————. "Sarah Orne Jewett and the Rich Tradition," *Colby Library Quarterly*, IV (November, 1957), 205-17. A letter—January 28, 1872—to her aunt Lucretia Fisk Perry concerns four persons who exerted influence upon SOJ's attitudes toward life and literature.

————. "Jewett's Cousins Charles and Charlie," *Colby Library Quarterly*, V (September, 1959), 48-58. SOJ's relationship with the male members of the Gilman family of Brunswick, Maine, with excerpts from unpublished letters.

————. "Jewett and the Gilman Women," *Colby Library Quarterly*, V (March, 1960), 94-103. Of the distaff side (see above), with excerpts from unpublished letters.

CHAPMAN, EDWARD M. "The New England of Sarah Orne Jewett," *Yale Review*, III (October, 1913), 157-72. SOJ's ancestry, residence, training, and experience permitted her to portray New England character, customs, flora, fauna, and weather with symbolic sureness.

FROST, JOHN ELDRIDGE. "The Letters of Sarah Orne Jewett," *Colby Library Quarterly*, V (September, 1959), 38-45. Serviceable check list of the locations of published and unpublished letters.

GEORGES, JUSTINE FLINT. "Mementoes of a Great Lady," *Shoreliner* (September, 1950), 10-14. Nostalgic reminiscence, with distinctive interior and exterior photographs of the Jewett house in South Berwick.

GRATTAN, C. HARTLEY. "Sarah Orne Jewett," *Bookman*, LXIX (May, 1929), 296-98. SOJ's art and historical value seen in her chronicle of the past and her influence on the present—Willa Cather.

GREEN, DAVID BONNELL. "Two Letters of Sarah Orne Jewett," *Notes & Queries*, New Series V (August, 1958), 361-62. To James Ripley Osgood—December 27, 1876—about Howells; to William Hayes Ward—August 14, [1881]—about a story for *The Independent*.

—————. "Sarah Orne Jewett's 'A Dark Night,' " *Papers of the Bibliographical Society of America*, LIII (4th Quarter, 1959), 331-34. A Letter to Arthur Stedman—February 25, 1895—demonstrating her urge to write historical narrative.

[HOWE, M. A. DE WOLFE.] "Sarah Orne Jewett," *Atlantic Monthly*, CIV (August, 1909), 280-81. Character sketch and critical summary of her place in American literature.

JEWETT, SARAH ORNE. "Looking Back on Girlhood," *Youth's Companion*, LXV (January 7, 1892), 5-6. Review of environment and personalities which "affected the course of my work as a writer."

LEVY, BABETTE MAY. "Mutations in New England Local Color," *New England Quarterly*, XIX (September, 1946), 338-58. Differences in light and shade exist within similarities of local color usages by Harriet Beecher Stowe, Mary E. Wilkins Freeman, Rose Terry Cooke, and SOJ.

LUCEY, WILLIAM L. "We New Englanders . . . ," *Records of the American Catholic Historical Society of Philadelphia*, LXX (March, June, 1959), 58-64. Seven letters of SOJ to Louise Imogen Guiney—November 6, 1894, to May 12 [1899].

NYE, GEORGE P. "Jewett and the Juvenile Critics," *Colby Library Quarterly*, V (September, 1959), 45-48. Two SOJ letters to Samuel Thurber—May 6, 21, 1906—about his students' reactions to her stories.

PARKER, JOHN AUSTIN. "Sarah Orne Jewett's 'Boat Song,' " *American Literature*, XXIII (March, 1951), 133-36. Corrects error in Weber *Bibliography*; establishes Richard Hoffman as composer of the music to "Boat Song."

SHACKFORD, MARTHA H. "Sarah Orne Jewett," *Sewanee Review*, XXX (January, 1922), 20-26. Overview of SOJ's accomplishment, touching on strong and weak points of her settings and characters.

SHORT, CLARICE. "Studies in Gentleness," *Western Humanities Review*, XI (Autumn, 1957), 387-93. Compares *The Country of the Pointed Firs* with Mrs. Gaskell's *Cranford*.

Selected Bibliography

SMITH, ELEANOR M. "The Literary Relationship of Sarah Orne Jewett and Willa Sibert Cather," *New England Quarterly*, XXIX (December, 1956), 472-92. Discusses differences in range and treatment; similarities in style, ideals, love of nature, and choice of protagonists.

THOMPSON, CHARLES MINER. "The Art of Miss Jewett," *Atlantic Monthly*, XCIV (October, 1904), 485-97. First consequential evaluation of SOJ; examines interaction of her Brahmin status and the New England democratic freedom of social intercourse.

TUTWILER, JULIA R. "Two New England Writers," *Gunton's Magazine*, XXV (November, 1903), 419-25. SOJ and Mary E. Wilkins Freeman are obliquely divergent realists: the former, sympathetically subjective; the latter, objectively detached.

WAGGONER, HYATT H. "The Unity of *The Country of the Pointed Firs*," *Twentieth Century Literature*, V (July, 1959), 67-73. Tone, setting, and theme provide unity; a symbolic pattern develops into a humanistic and religious vision of life.

WEBER, CARL J. "Whittier and Sarah Orne Jewett," *New England Quarterly*, XVIII (September, 1945), 401-7. Erroneous statement that SOJ's "The Eagle Trees" is here published for the first time is acknowledged in the *Bibliography*, page 81.

————. "Sarah Orne Jewett's First Story," *New England Quarterly*, XIX (March, 1946), 85-90. Publication of "Jenny Garrow's Lovers" in *The Flag of Our Union*, January 18, 1868.

————. "New England Through French Eyes Fifty Years Ago," *New England Quarterly*, XX (September, 1947), 385-96. Visit by SOJ and the French writer Thérèse Blanc-Bentzon to the Shaker Colony in Alfred, Maine, in June, 1897.

Index

Aldrich, Thomas Bailey, 11, 12, 25, 26, 99, 116
Arnold, Matthew, 21, 25
Atlantic Monthly, 11, 24, 26, 54, 65, 66, 87, 91, 97, 132
Austen, Jane, 19, 21, 88

Balzac, Honoré de, 21
Bentzon, Th. (Marie Thérèse Blanc), 26
Brooks, Van Wyck, 158, 162
Browning, Robert, 97, 113
Burns, Robert, 115

Cather, Willa, 11, 26, 27, 59, 61, 80, 89, 133, 158, 160-61, 162, 163
Cervantes, 21
Chekhov, Anton, 51
Civil War, 16, 17, 28, 129, 132
Coolidge, Susan, 26
Crane, Stephen, 60, 117

Darwin, Charles, 70, 73
Dickens, Charles, 25, 109, 140
Dickinson, Emily, 64
Du Maurier, George, 12, 25

Eliot, George, 21, 58
Embargo of 1807, 15, 16, 17, 20
Emerson, Ralph Waldo, 11, 21, 28, 55, 59, 70, 142, 158

Faulkner, William, 35, 158
Fielding, Henry, 21, 133
Fields, Annie, 11-12, 19, 25, 27, 35, 101
Fields, James T., 11, 24, 25, 26
Flaubert, Gustave, 21, 35, 51, 52, 60, 89
Freeman, Mary E. Wilkins, 60, 101

Frost, John Eldridge, 33, 160, 163
Frost, Robert, 75, 158

Gaskell, Mrs. Elizabeth, 35
Guiney, Louise Imogen, 26, 51

Hardy, Thomas, 35, 60
Harte, Bret, 77, 94
Hawthorne, Nathaniel, 51, 53, 65, 78, 84, 97-98, 99, 105, 107, 116, 149, 158
Hazlitt, William, 65, 76
Henry, O., 50
Historical romances, 152
Holmes, Oliver Wendell, 11, 26, 28
Howe, Julia Ward, 26
Howe, M. A. DeWolfe, 60, 156, 161, 162
Howells, William Dean, 11, 19, 24, 26, 48, 51, 60, 61, 63, 65, 132, 138, 158

Irving, Washington, 97, 120, 158

James, Henry, 11, 12, 25, 29, 60, 87, 89, 92, 133, 152, 158, 161
Jewett, Sarah Orne, *passim;* characters, 38-41, 52-58; children's stories, 32, 155-56; history, 156-57; life and times, 11-12, 15-29; locale, 36-38; novels, 131-54; point of view, 61-63; pseudonyms, 11, 24; realism, 30-35, 58-61, 66-67; reputation, 157-59; short stories, 87-130; sketches, 65-80, 86; sketch-stories, 80-86; style, 48-52; techniques, 63-64; themes, 41-47; verse, 156

WRITINGS OF:

"All My Sad Captains," 36, 39, 50, 112

"Andrew's Fortune," 43, 58, 117-18

"Aunt Cynthy Dallett," 39, 75, 109-10, 124

"Autumn Holiday, An," 39, 58, 80-82, 115, 119, 147

Betty Leicester, 25, 34, 46, 155

Betty Leicester's Christmas, 155

"Between Mass and Vespers," 45, 53, 89, 127-28

"Bit of Shore Life, A," 38, 39, 53, 57, 62, 66, 67-69

"Bold Words at the Bridge," 51, 128

"By the Morning Boat," 12, 31, 39, 42, 53, 55, 58, 117, 157

"Business Man, A," 45, 126

"Confession of a House-Breaker, The," 31, 75-76

"Coon Dog, The," 50, 96

Country By-Ways, 11, 19, 21, 66, 71, 160, 161

Country Doctor, A, 12, 21, 31, 34, 39, 40, 43, 44, 45, 46, 47, 53, 54, 55, 58, 63, 131, 138-41, 143, 160

Country of the Pointed Firs, The, 12, 29, 31, 36, 38, 39, 40, 48, 49, 55, 56, 57, 58, 60, 62, 66, 86, 103, 110, 130, 131, 133, 137, 144-52, 157, 158, 159

"Courting of Sister Wisby, The," 31, 50, 58, 63, 82-84, 95, 110

"Decoration Day," 49, 53, 124-25

Deephaven, 11, 17, 20, 23, 24, 26, 29, 31, 32, 34, 36, 39, 40, 41, 45, 50, 51, 52, 53, 57, 58, 60, 62, 63, 66, 70, 129, 130, 132-38, 145, 146, 147, 149, 151, 157, 160, 161, 163

"Dulham Ladies, The," 12, 39, 42, 44, 49, 51, 58, 62, 82, 114-16, 130, 131, 157

"Eagle Trees, The," 26

Empty Purse, An, 31, 44, 45, 124

"Failure of David Berry, The," 32, 39, 42, 49, 126

"Fair Day," 39, 46, 53, 55, 106-7

"Fame's Little Day," 44, 92-93, 115

"Farmer Finch," 32, 38, 39, 55, 82, 118-19

"Flight of Betsey Lane, The," 39, 45, 49, 51, 106, 107-8, 109, 157

"From a Mournful Villager," 42, 74-75

"Going to Shrewsbury," 44, 113

"Good Luck: A Girl's Story," 41, 58

"Gray Man, The," 41, 53, 96, 98-99, 146, 163

"Gray Mills of Farley, The," 127

"Guests of Mrs. Timms, The," 12, 31, 51, 75, 108-9, 110, 157

"Hiltons' Holiday, The," 42, 121-22, 157

"In Dark New England Days," 39, 49, 54, 116

"Jenny Garrow's Lovers," 11, 24, 87, 90-91, 130

King of Folly Island and Other People, The, 26

"King of Folly Island, The," 32, 39, 40, 46, 49, 62, 120-21, 126, 148

"Lady Ferry," 70, 79, 96, 97-98, 163

"Landless Farmer, A," 35, 42, 58, 60, 63, 121, 123

"Landscape Chamber, The," 40, 42, 46, 49, 54, 84-86, 96, 105, 146

"Late Supper, A," 34, 45, 49, 51, 113

"Law Lane," 34, 58, 104-5, 124

Life of Nancy, The, 108

"Life of Nancy, The," 31, 38, 45, 46, 62, 119-20

"Little Captive Maid, A," 41, 62, 128

"Little French Mary," 31, 42, 128

"Little Traveler, A," 40, 49, 76-77

"Looking Back on Girlhood," 24, 160

"Lost Lover, A," 40, 46, 58, 103, 110

"Luck of the Bogans, The," 41, 50, 56, 127

Marsh Island, A, 39, 46, 49, 50,

52, 55, 57, 58, 131, 141-44, 151, 153
"Marsh Rosemary," 39, 49, 50 57, 110, 113-14, 119, 157
"Martha's Lady," 51
"Mary and Martha," 39, 44, 124
"Mate of the Daylight, The," 50, 58, 118
"Mère Pochette," 128
"Miss Becky's Pilgrimage," 46, 47, 63, 110, 122
"Miss Debby's Neighbors," 50, 94-95
"Miss Esther's Guest," 46, 55, 111, 157
"Miss Peck's Promotion," 31, 39, 46, 53, 103-4, 107, 110, 112
"Miss Sydney's Flowers," 40, 46, 49, 56, 58, 87, 100
"Miss Tempy's Watchers," 12, 53, 57, 105-6, 156, 157
"Mistress of Sydenham Plantation, The," 70, 79, 129
"Mr. Bruce," 11, 24, 52, 58, 87, 91
"Native of Winby, A," 30, 58, 63, 123-24
"Neighbor's Landmark, A," 31, 46, 56, 75, 96, 100-1, 124
"New Parishioner, A," 46, 55, 58, 63, 110, 122-23
"News from Petersham, The," 50, 95
"Night Before Thanksgiving, The," 32, 45, 49, 53, 58, 124
"October Ride, An," 56, 71-74
"Only Rose, The," 46, 50, 110, 112-13
"Only Son, An," 42, 46, 118
"Passing of Sister Barsett, The," 50, 95-96, 104
Play Days, 155-56
"Queen's Twin, The," 38, 40, 49, 86, 148
"Quest of Mr. Teaby, The," 39, 46, 50, 53, 57, 110-11
"River Driftwood," 17, 45, 55, 69-70
"Second Spring, A," 39, 46, 53, 55, 111-12

"Shore House, The," 65
"Sorrowful Guest, A," 91-92
Story of the Normans, The, 20, 156-57
Strangers and Wayfarers, 12, 52, 87
"Taking of Captain Ball, The," 39, 46, 50, 62, 111-12
Tales of New England, 87
"Tom's Husband," 50, 82, 119, 125-26
Tory Lover, The, 12, 26, 29, 39, 43, 53, 86, 89, 96, 131, 152-54
"Town Poor, The," 12, 32, 39, 49, 114, 157
"Two Browns, The," 46, 50, 126
Verses, 156
"Village Shop, A," 39, 40, 42, 49, 50, 105
"War Debt, A," 62, 92, 129-30
"Where's Nora?" 128
White Heron and Other Stories, A, 29, 52, 88, 163
"White Heron, A," 12, 38, 44, 46, 55, 62, 101-3, 146, 156, 157
"White Rose Road, The," 77-80, 146
"Winter Courtship, A," 50, 53, 111
"Winter Drive, A," 31, 56, 71, 75
Jewett, Theodore Furber, 20
Jewett, Theodore Herman, 20-21, 81
Johnson, Samuel, 21, 47

Kipling, Rudyard, 12, 25, 108, 144

Lamb, Charles, 65, 75
Lee, Vernon, 26
Local-color writing, 17-18, 52, 94
Longfellow, Henry Wadsworth, 11, 19, 26, 28
Lowell, James Russell, 11, 21, 26, 28, 52, 63-64

Magazine editors, 26
Mather, Cotton, 69
Matthiessen, F. O., 33, 48, 59, 64, 106, 149, 158, 160, 161, 162, 163
Maupassant, Guy de, 51

Index

Melville, Herman, 126
Meynell, Alice, 26
Millet, Jean François, 54, 142
Milton, John, 21
Mitchell, S. Weir, 101
Montaigne, 21

Oliphant, Mrs. Margaret, 21
O'Neill, Eugene, 121

Parrington, Vernon L., 33, 161
Pattee, Fred L., 28, 59, 66, 101, 138
Perry, Dr. William, 20, 25
Phelps, Elizabeth Stuart, *see* Ward, E. S. P.
Plato, 17, 58-59, 132
Poe, Edgar Allan, 58, 84-85, 86, 87, 92, 97, 99, 116

Quinn, Arthur Hobson, 101, 138, 144, 149

Radcliffe, Anne, 84
Reade, Charles, 12, 25
Robinson, E. A., 104, 158
Rossetti, Christina, 12, 25
Ruskin, John, 71

Scott, Walter, 88, 153
Scudder, Horace E., 11, 26, 65, 89, 131, 152
Shakespeare, 35, 50, 58, 73, 104, 121, 144, 148
Smollett, Tobias, 21
Spofford, Harriet Preston, 26

Steinbeck, John, 117, 158
Sterne, Laurence, 21
Stevenson, R. L., 65, 76, 104
Stowe, Harriet Beecher, 11, 23, 26, 29, 132, 158, 160
Swift, Jonathan, 98

Taine, Hippolyte, 15
Tennyson, Alfred, 12, 21, 25
Terry, Ellen, 101
Thackeray, Anne, 25, 49
Thaxter, Celia, 26, 28
Thompson, Charles Miner, 33, 46, 88, 131
Thoreau, H. D., 27, 56, 150, 158
Tolstoi, Leo, 21, 101
Turgenev, Ivan, 21, 33, 60
Turner, Frederick Jackson, 74
Twain, Mark, 12, 25, 81, 94, 96, 104, 158

Ward, E. S. P., 28, 138
Ward, Mrs. Humphry, 12, 25
Warner, Charles Dudley, 26, 152
Wharton, Edith, 158
Whitman, Sarah Wyman, 25, 54, 160
Whitman, Walt, 45, 158
Whittier, John Greenleaf, 11, 26, 28, 68, 132
Wordsworth, Dorothy, 51
Wordsworth, William, 43, 58-59, 60, 100

Zola, Emile, 21, 60